A PRIMER
FOR
ANGRY CHRISTIANS

Steve Clapp
Sue Ingels Mauck

CHRIST

COVENANT

CHANGE

COMMUNITY

Reverend Steve Clapp
C-4 RESOURCES
P.O. Box 27
Sidell, Illinois 61876

Biblical quotations, unless otherwise indicated, are from the Revised Standard Version of the Bible.

Drawings are by E. Jane Clapp and Eunice Buck. Photographs are by Dave Lafary, Bert Whittier, and Steve Clapp.

Printing and assembly was done by Crouse Printing of Champaign, Illinois. Special appreciation is expressed to David Crouse, Shirley Crouse, Steve Askins, Sonnie Schrock, Gerry Burdette, Ralph Crabtree, Ed Anderson, and Roger Bickers.

CONTENTS

USING THIS BOOK

This book has been designed for use in a variety of ways:
- As a resource for personal reading and growth.
- As a resource for weekend retreat groups.
- As a resource for on-going local church classes and groups.
- As a resource for summer camps.
- As a resource for short-term local church classes and groups.

The book has two parts. The first part has a total of four chapters which discuss issues related to anger and power. There are subtopics to each of those chapters, and each chapter concludes with several activities FOR YOU TO DO as an individual or with a group. The second part provides four weeks of activity including daily Bible study and journal writing. The second part of the book should give you significant help applying what you learn in the first part of the book.

If you are reading the book by yourself, you can read the first part at whatever rate you wish. The second part will be best if spread over four weeks of time and if the daily activities are completed. Even if you are reading the book on your own, you may find it helpful to discuss many of the issues with other people.

The FOR YOU TO DO sections contain a large number of activity possibilities. The first day of each week in the journal section contains suggestions for group discussion. Thus several approaches to covering the material with a class or group are available:
- Spend twelve weeks on the study. Use two sessions for each of the four chapters in the first part. Then have group members work on the daily activities and devotions of the second part over a period of four weeks, and spend group time discussing the questions for the first day of each week.
- Cover the first part at a retreat or camp setting, and then have group members continue the second part over a four week period. They can continue the work individually, or you can have a weekly meeting to go over the first day's questions each week.
- Meet for two hours a week for four weeks to cover the first part of the book. Then meet an hour a week for the next four weeks to cover the second part of the book.

There obviously are other options! The book has been designed to be flexible. We do recommend that, whether you are working as an individual or in a group, you spend a full four weeks on the second part of the book. Also note that some of the simulation games can be very time consuming—depending on how involved you want to become.

We pray that this book will help you deal more effectively as a Christian with issues of anger, power, justice, and love.

—Steve Clapp and Sue Ingels Mauck

PART I.

CHAPTER ONE

THE RIGHT TO BE ANGRY

Violent expressions of anger are common in our society and generally constitute the most spectacular stories of the daily newspaper.

- Following a winter storm, a snow plow driver in Chicago went berserk and began running the plow into the sides of parked autmobiles. Witnesses and victims climbed into cars and trucks and pursued him onto an interstate highway. Before his apprehension by the police, the driver killed one of those following him.

- Farmers, normally opposed to violence and civil disobedience, clogged the highways of Washington, D.C., with tractors as they sought public recognition and legislative change in the face of prices which would not meet their expenses. Several persons were injured in violent confrontations precipitated by the protest. Emergency vehicles had difficulty maneuvering past the tractors.

- An outwardly calm and reserved man planned and carried out the execution of several homosexuals in San Francisco. One of his stray bullets killed a small child.

- A woman in Denver murdered her husband and children with a knife. She left a message written in their blood and then killed herself.

Protestants and Catholics fight in Ireland. Whites and Blacks fight in Africa. Religious and political power struggles continue to plague Iran. The world is not at peace.

While most of us are not participants in such violence, we are nevertheless aware of that part of ourselves which might be capable of violence. Both we and those close to us have said or thought such things as:

- "He doesn't have a right to live."
- "I can forgive a lot of things, but I can't forgive what she did to me."
- "I'll make him pay for that if it takes the rest of my life."
- "Sometimes I just want to slam my car into people who drive like that."
- "I hate her so much that I can't think straight."
- "That's the kind of person I can't stand."
- "No court in the country would convict her if she murdered him."

Those are not the words of diabolical, evil people. Those are the words of normal, rational people—we think!

Most churches have not addressed the topic of ANGER in ways which have been especially helpful to those struggling to live as Christians. According to some views, the words *anger* and *Christian* are mutually exclusive—a Christian, by definition, cannot be a person of anger. Many churches have popularized the image of Jesus as gentle, meek, and mild. Sunday School literature emphasizes the Biblical teachings against anger and against the violence which often accompanies anger. The Christian person is depicted as one who either has sufficient self-control to never be angry or has sufficient guilt to seek God's forgiveness for passing moments of anger.

Some other religious perspectives accept the reality of anger and do not suggest that people should feel guilty over feelings of anger. The major focus from this perspective is on control of one's actions: "It's all right to feel angry, BUT be sure that you don't act on that anger."

The Bible certainly does emphasize the importance of meekness, gentleness, and forgiveness in human relationships. While the Bible contains examples of violence, the overall thrust of Scripture condemns violent solutions to problems between people or nations. Yet the Old Testament clearly speaks at times of a God of wrath and anger. In Genesis, God sends a flood to destroy most of humanity because of the wickedness which God has observed. The prophets speak of God's anger over the disobedience of the Hebrew people. Proverbs speaks of God's displeasure with those who take advantage of the poor. In the New Testament, Jesus speaks of love and forgiveness but also throws the money changers out of the temple.

SO—there are no easy answers. Anger is an emotion common to all people and is very much part of our lives. In this book, we plan to explore together a number of important issues for Christian people. The topic is complex, because it is not possible to study anger without also looking at the issues of assertiveness, aggression, power, violence, justice, and love. Thus the Bible has a great deal to say about anger and about issues related to anger. We'll be trying to give you exposure to what the Scriptures say; to what modern psychology says; to the full range of options in dealing with these issues; and to some practical handles for improving the quality of your own life.

And God said to Noah, "I have determined to make an end of all flesh; for the earth is filled with violence through them; behold, I will destroy them with the earth. . . . . Behold, I will bring a flood of waters upon the earth, to destroy all flesh in which is the breath of life from under heaven."   Genesis 6:13, 17a.

GET OUT!

And Jesus entered the temple of God and drove out all who sold and bought in the temple, and he overturned the tables of the money-changers and the seats of those who sold pigeons. Matthew 21:12.

THE SCRIPTURES
ON ANGER AND POWER

GENESIS 7:23. "He blotted out every living thing that was upon the face of the ground, man and animals and creeping things and birds of the air; they were blotted out from the earth. Only Noah was left, and those that were with him in the ark."

EXODUS 32:19. "And as soon as he came near the camp and saw the calf and the dancing, Moses' anger burned hot, and he threw the tables out of his hands and broke them at the foot of the mountain."

EXODUS 11:33. "While the meat was yet between their teeth, before it was consumed, the anger of the Lord was kindled against the people; and the Lord smote the people with a very great plague."

DEUTERONOMY 5:17. "You shall not kill."

2 KINGS 17:18. "Therefore the Lord was very angry with Israel, and removed them out of his sight; none was left but the tribe of Judah alone."

NEHEMIAH 9:17b. "But thou art a God ready to forgive, gracious and merciful, slow to anger and abounding in steadfast love, and didst not forsake them."

PROVERBS 15:1. "A soft answer turns away wrath, but a harsh word stirs up anger."

PROVERBS 25:21-22. "If your enemy is hungry, give him bread to eat; and if he is thirsty, give him water to drink; for you will heap coals of fire on his head, and the Lord will reward you."

PROVERBS 26:3. "A whip for the horse, a bridle for the ass, and a rod for the back of fools."

AMOS 2:6-7a. "Thus says the Lord: 'For three transgressions of Israel, and for four, I will not revoke the punishment; because they sell the righteous for silver, and the needy for a pair of shoes - that they trample the head of the poor into the dust of the earth, and turn aside the way of the afflicted.' "

MATTHEW 5:22. "But I say to you that every one who is angry with his brother shall be liable to judgment; whoever insults his brother shall be liable to the council, and whoever says, 'You fool!' shall be liable to the hell of fire."

MATTHEW 5:39. "But I say to you, Do not resist one who is evil. But if any one strikes you on the right cheek, turn to him the other also."

MARK 3:5. "And he [Jesus] looked around at them with anger, grieved at their hardness of heart, and said to the man, 'Stretch out your hand.' He stretched it out, and his hand was restored."

LUKE 10:27. " 'You shall love the Lord your God with all your heart, and with all your soul, and with all your strength, and with all your mind; and your neighbor as yourself.' "

JOHN 2:15. "And making a whip of cords, he [Jesus] drove them all, with the sheep and oxen, out of the temple; and he poured out the coins of the money-changers and overturned their tables."

EPHESIANS 5:26. "Be angry but do not sin; do not let the sun go down on your anger."

JAMES 1:19. "Know this, my beloved brethren. Let every man be quick to hear, slow to speak, slow to anger, for the anger of man does not work the righteousness of God."

1 JOHN 4:20. "If any one says, 'I love God,' and hates his brother, he is a liar; for he who does not love his brother whom he has seen, cannot love God whom he has not seen."

ANGER, ASSERTIVENESS, AND AGGRESSION

ANGER is an emotion. Anger is a feeling of hostility or disgust toward physical objects, the nature of life, other persons, or yourself. Other words sometimes used as substitutes for anger are ire, rage, indignation, fury, and wrath. Those words all suggest varying degrees of intensity of feeling. ALL OF US EXPERIENCE ANGER. In a C-4 RESOURCES study of youth views on anger and power, 100% of the six hundred teenagers responding said that they experienced strong feelings of anger at least part of the time and that they often did not cope well with their anger. In a separate study of college age people (involving 170 people in their late teens and early twenties), 70% felt that they deal constructively with anger half the time or less. So—you are not alone in experiencing frustration about the best way to deal with anger. You may be angry at your parents; at teachers; at a brother or sister; at the driver who cuts in front of you on the way to school; at a car that won't start; at a pencil that breaks; or at yourself for making a bad decision. We all experience such feelings.

AGGRESSION is not the same as anger. Aggression is a more dominating style of relating to other people. An aggressive person often overlooks the rights of others in an effort at personal gain. While aggression is often motivated by feelings of anger, aggression itself is an action rather than a feeling. You don't have to be aggressive simply because you feel angry.

ASSERTIVENESS differs from both anger and aggression. Assertiveness is a basically positive style which means insuring that your rights and the rights of others are recognized—but does not mean violating the rights of others. Many people who act with aggression toward others would be better off if they learned how to be assertive instead. An assertive person works to avoid being a doormat for others but, unlike the aggressive person, also avoids using others as a doormat.

In each of the following situations, try to decide which is the example of anger; the example of aggression; and the example of assertiveness.

SAMPLE: Sally orders a hamburger "well done" at a restaurant. She very much dislikes eating meat which still appears red. When the waiter serves her hamburger, Sally readily sees that the meat is not well done. Sally can respond in these ways:

A. *Aggressive.* Sally snarls at the waiter, "I'm not going to eat this garbage. I wanted my food well done. This cow is still alive. I'm not paying for this mess."

B. *Anger.* Sally felt sick to her stomach from looking at the bleeding hamburger and also was mad. She knew that she had clearly ordered the food well done. She also knew that she couldn't stand to eat it unless it was cooked longer.

C. *Assertive.* As soon as the food has been served, Sally says to the waiter, "I'm sorry, but I can't eat that hamburger. I wanted the hamburger well done, and this one is too rare for me. I'd appreciate it if you had it cooked a little longer or brought me a new one."

A is an aggressive response. While Sally has every right to be upset and to not pay for food which she can't eat, this response is not a good one. First, Sally's aggressiveness violates the rights of the waiter. The waiter did not intentionally bring her something which she couldn't eat. The error could have been caused by a careless chef; by the waiter not writing down the order properly; or by the waiter picking up the wrong order. But the waiter did not INTEND to serve bad food to Sally, and Sally's response is too strong. Second, Sally's bold proclamation that she won't pay for the mess doesn't help her get food that she can eat. It would be better to work on a solution to the problem before refusing payment. Third, Sally herself is bound to feel guilty later for having been so nasty to the waiter. It's hard to feel good about yourself when you're unkind to others.

B is an angry response. It's very hard to avoid not being angry when faced with food that is repulsive. Trying to ignore the feeling of anger will probably not be helpful. What is important is trying to deal with the anger in a helpful way. Sally would probably have chosen response *A* because she is angry. We've already indicated why that response is not a good one. If Sally says nothing, however, she'll have to sit through the meal resenting the bloody hamburger or eat it in spite of her dislike for it. There is another option . . .

C is an assertive response. Sally does not intend to suffer in silence or to pay for food which she can't eat. She also recognizes that being discourteous to the waiter is not a proper response and may also not be a helpful response. She simply states the problem as courteously as possible and suggests a way of resolving it.

It takes little imagination to understand which of the responses is most likely to result in Sally's enjoying the meal and in her showing the waiter the same respect which she would expect in his place. From a Christian perspective, being assertive always involves "doing unto others as you would have them do unto you."

SITUATION 2: Pete's father has let him use the car every weekend, but Pete has been violating their mutually accepted rule that he will be home by midnight. He has been coming home at 1:30 A.M. and 2:00 A.M. most of the time. His father finally lays down the law and says that Pete will be grounded if he is later than midnight one more time. Although Pete is a little angry about the situation, he also recognizes that he has knowingly violated the rule, so he decides to reform.

Unfortunately, he has a flat tire on the way home; has trouble changing the tire; and ends up not getting home until 2:00 A.M. His father is waiting for him and informs him that he is grounded for the next month. Pete can respond in these ways:

A. _____ . Pete feels his stomach tightening and his skin flushing. He is in a rage. He had been trying very, very hard to be home on time. Then he had to have a flat tire on that night of all nights, and his father didn't give him a chance to explain. It seems to Pete that it doesn't even pay to try to do the right thing.

B. _____ . Pete asks his father if they can sit down and talk about it. Then Pete says, "I know that I violated the rule again, and I really am sorry. I do want you to know that the reason I was late tonight was that I had a flat tire on the way home. The tire's still in the trunk of the car. I had left the restaurant in time to be here by midnight, and I'd made my mind up that I was going to break the pattern of being late. I know that I'm still in violation of the rule, and I understand that I probably should have left early enough not to be so close on time. But I just didn't expect a flat tire, and I had a lot of trouble changing it. A month is a long time to be grounded. I don't blame you for being so unhappy with me, but I wish we could work something else out."

C. _____ . Pete threw the car keys on the floor and yelled at his father, "Blast it! It's not fair! I tried! I really tried. This is the first time that I've really made a big effort to be home on time, and this is the time that you get tough with me. It's not my fault that I had the flat."

The responses and their consequences are fairly obvious. Response *A* is anger, and almost anyone in Pete's situation would feel anger. But the way of coping with that anger will probably make a lot of difference in what happens to Pete. Response *B* is an assertive response, and it is the one which is most likely to help the relationship between Pete and his father. While Pete no doubt hopes that his father will change his mind about the month's grounding, he also recognizes that his father has a right to be upset—and he tells his father that he understands why he is upset. He also shares the reason for his being late this time. As the discussion continues, his father may not let him off without any punishment, but it may be that the penalty will be reduced. In any event, Pete will have expressed his feelings rather than keeping them bottled up; and the relationship with his father should be improved.

SITUATION 3: Kim and Tom are on their fourth date together. Both of them are juniors in high school and enjoy being together. They kissed briefly before Kim went inside her house on the first and second dates. On the third date, they necked for awhile in the car. Now Tom has begun to stroke Kim's body and wants to move into the back seat. Things are moving too fast for Kim. She is physically excited by Tom, but she doesn't feel ready to move into the back seat. She can respond in three ways:

A. _____ . Kim pushes Tom away and opens the car door. "I'm not ready for this, and you wouldn't do it if you respected me. You can't take me to a movie and then expect me to climb into your back seat. You may be cheap, but I'm not."

B. _____ . Kim pulls back a little from Tom and says, "I need to talk about it before we do anything more. Part of me wants your hands all over me and wants to get into the back seat. But that makes another part of me feel cheap and dirty and mad. I like you, but I wasn't planning on the physical part going this fast. I sat close to you at the movie, and I may have given you the impression that I wanted to go faster than I do. We need to talk more about this."

C. _____ . Although part of Kim feels physically aroused and would like to move into the back seat, another part of her feels like Tom is just using her. After all, he paid for the expenses of the date. It makes her feel like Tom believes he can buy her body by asking her out. She also recognizes that she may have encouraged him by sitting so tight against him at the movie, and she feels mad at herself because of that.

Response *C* is anger. Given the situation and feeling uncertain about how far she wants to go in physical affection, Kim can hardly help feeling angry. Part of her anger is directed at herself for perhaps having encouraged Tom more than she should have. If Kim does not move to one of the other responses, she will end up doing more sexually than she actually wants and may be even more angry with herself and Tom afterwards.

Response *A* is an aggressive response. It certainly stops the sexual activity. It may, however, be too strong a response. Kim does not acknowledge in this response that she may have given encouragement to Tom which she didn't actually mean. This response will probably end their relationship, and that may be a shame if Kim genuinely likes Tom.

Response *B* is an assertive response. Kim stops the activity, and then proceeds to share her feelings. She acknowledges her own responsibility for what they are doing and asks Tom to talk about it. This response is the most likely one to preserve the relationship and to help them build respect for each other.

The next chapter will provide some further examples of ways to deal with anger. Assertiveness and aggressiveness are not the only ways, and the appropriate way often depends on the situation. All of these instances, however, are ones in which an assertive approach was the most likely way to help all concerned. Anger, aggression, and assertiveness are so frequently confused, that we wanted you to better understand the distinction early in the book.

ANGER, POWER, AND VIOLENCE

Anger, power, and violence are related concepts. ***POWER is not an emotion. It can perhaps best be viewed as the ability to cause change in the world, in other people, or in yourself.*** All people have some power. For example:

- Physical strength provides the power to move objects; to achieve athletically; and sometimes to force others to do as one wishes.

- Intelligence is a form of power, since it lets us solve problems; better understand the world in which we live; organize our lives; and cope with life.

- The possession of money provides a great deal of power in our society, and many conflicts in our society are the result of some persons having a great deal more money than others.

$50,000 (plus)
per year

$10,000 (plus-minus)
per year

$5000 (minus)
per year

- The opportunity to help or hurt, to frustrate or assist other persons is also a form of power.

- Having friends and loved ones is a form of power. When our opinions and our affection are important to another person, we gain a certain measure of power (or ability to influence or control).

- Knowledge can be a strong form of power. Knowing how to repair a car when others do not is a form of power; knowing how to sew or cook can be a form of power; knowing the secrets of another person can be a form of power.

Obviously all the kinds of power listed above (as well as some other kinds of power which you may be able to think of) can be used to HELP others and to make life more enjoyable or can be used to HURT others and to make life miserable.

VIOLENCE occurs when power is used to hurt another individual or a group of individuals. Violence almost always occurs because people are very angry and choose to use their power in a destructive way.

We often think of physical power when we think of violence. Crimes of violence are a major problem in most parts of the United States and Canada. It is also discouraging to know that a large percentage of violent crimes are committed by teenagers.

But there are other forms of violence. Some of these forms of violence are directed against individuals; others are directed at whole groups of people. All of the following are considered (by at least some Christian people) as acts of violence:

- Attacks on the self-worth of others. "I hate you." "I don't want anything to do with you." "I can't stand being around you." "Leave me alone. I don't want any part of you." "You act like a slut."

- Ignoring other people. Avoiding contact with people of another race or with people who are physically handicapped or with people who have different religious beliefs or values. This kind of avoidance can be very painful to a person who feels lonely and insecure.

- Countries which have large quantities of food refusing to share adequate resources with countries which have high levels of starvation and malnutrition.

- Charging and billing practices of medical facilities and state agencies which result in inadequate medical and dental care for persons with very limited financial resources.

- Hiring practices of businesses and industries which discriminate against persons on the basis of race, physical handicaps, or age.

- Sharing malicious gossip about others. "I heard that she. . . ." "You'll never believe what he did. . . ." "It may not be true, but a good friend of mine told me that they. . . ." "People would sure avoid them if they knew that. . . ." "Do you know what she did in the shopping center? . . ." "Did you hear what went on at that party? . . ."

As you can see, "violence" can refer to a broad range of activities. While anger is not always the motivation for acts of violence, anger is often involved. Some people believe that our inability to handle anger in a satisfactory way is part of the reason that we are insensitive to the needs of others— that we ignore others because we are so involved in our own problems. That is not an acceptable attitude for a Christian.

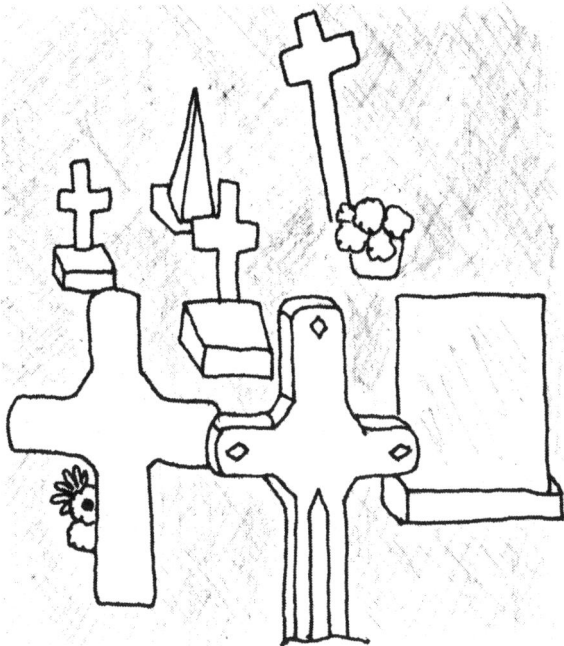

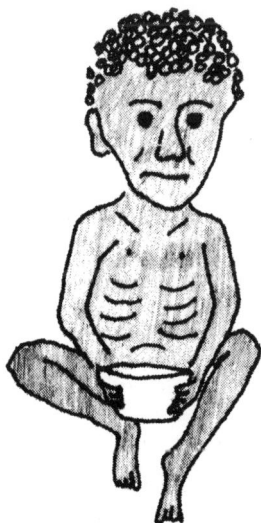

Violence can take many forms. But destruction and suffering are the result.

DO WE HAVE A RIGHT TO BE ANGRY?

Whether we have a "right" to be angry or not, it certainly is true that all of us experience feelings of anger. While being a Christian has some strong implications for how we deal with anger, one cannot escape the reality of anger in our world. Anger is clearly related to issues of power and violence in our world. An unhealthy view of anger and the inability to properly channel or direct that anger have a number of consequences at the individual level, in relationships, in the church, and in society as a whole.

Christian people often feel guilt as a result of their feelings of anger. In the C-4 RESOURCES survey of teenagers, 93% expressed agreement with the statement: "A Christian person should be able to control his or her anger." In that same sample, 69% expressed agreement with the statement: "A mature Christian does not have feelings of anger." Yet 100% of those persons acknowledged that they had feelings of anger—and that those feelings were sometimes intense! The conflict between believing that a Christian should not be angry and the reality of *being angry* can produce a lot of guilt.

As you may have noted when you did the exercises in ANGER, ASSERTIVENESS, AND AGGRESSION, repressing anger completely often results in our being taken advantage of by others—thus we go through life as the doormats for the feet of others. Many persons adopt a "victim" lifestyle which permits or even encourages others to take advantage of them. Persons who turn their anger inward because of guilt may in time develop physical symptoms including ulcers, migraine, heart difficulty, and nervous disorders.

Relationships cannot be at their best if anger is a major problem for even one person in the relationship. Most of us are familiar with the damage done by outwardly hostile people who lose their tempers frequently, provoke conflict, and escalate minor disagreements to the level of open war. Harm is also done by those who remain silent in the face of obvious injustice rather than risk confrontation with another's anger.

Our lack of willingness to even talk about anger in the Christian community causes many problems for the church. People feel that they must be *nice, proper, and controlled* within the church. Real feelings are often hidden. Some persons become skilled at giving the outward appearance of concern and benevolence while continuously hurting others by gossip and innuendo. Church groups become unwilling to deal with internal differences of opinion; and a forceful, vocal minority may inflict their will on a silent majority who wish to avoid conflict at any cost. Such churches will not risk public stands on unpopular issues because acceptance, harmony, and new member appeal become more important than justice and Christian proclamation.

Similar problems afflict our society. Government officials and political figures learn that justice is not so important as popularity and that some issues should be avoided. Groups which display anger over presumed injustice are quickly put in their place if their power base is weak or placated if their power base is strong.

Our difficulty in understanding or handling anger relates to problems in other areas. As previously indicated, anger, power, and violence are related concepts. Power, however, is also related to JUSTICE and to LOVE. In the world in which we live, there can be no justice for individuals or groups unless there is power to enforce that justice. From the Christian perspective, justice which is not rooted in love is not justice at all.

If one proceeds on the assumption that the Creator knew His craft in the design of humanity, then what is the purpose of the anger which is so common to all people? Is that emotion given to us only as a temptation to be overcome? Or is that emotion, properly channeled, what motivates us to use our God-given power to obtain justice for ourselves and others—justice which is grounded in the love of God?

The chapters which follow should help you better deal with the issues related not only to anger, power, and violence—but also with the issues that grow out of Christ's concern for justice and love. You have a RIGHT to be angry, but none of us has a right to express that anger in whatever way we choose. How we handle our feelings of anger may be one of the most important issues in life for a Christian person and for the survival of the world in which we live.

FOR YOU TO DO

This section of each chapter will include several activities which you may find helpful to do—either by yourself or with others. If you are sharing this book as a part of a class or fellowship group study, you may often not have enough time to do all the activities. Some of the suggestions will be for long term projects that involve a great deal of commitment and effort. Others can easily be done within the space of a regular group meeting.

ACTIVITY #1: Look at the box which is titled THE SCRIPTURES ON ANGER AND POWER. These quotations obviously were taken out of context. Pick out some of the statements which are of particular interest to you, and then look up in your Bible the entire context of the verse or verses. You will usually need to read at least the paragraph in which the verse(s) appeared. Note that the situations to which these verses were directed are not identical. Thus we should not be surprised that some parts of Scripture put greater emphasis on God's judgment (or even anger!) while others put greater emphasis on His justice and forgiveness.

It is also important to recognize that the Scriptures are a record of God's dealing with humanity—and that our perceptions of God have gone through some change. Thus some Old Testament teachings need to be put in tension with the New Testament words and actions of Christ.

As you continue in this book, you will have opportunity for more intensive study of many passages of Scripture. Do not worry about complete understanding of so many verses of Scripture at this point. The purpose of this activity is to expose you to the broad range of Biblical counsel on issues of anger and power.

ACTIVITY #2: Look at your own attitudes about anger and power. Indicate the extent of your agreement or disagreement with the statements which follow by using these symbols:

SA = Strongly Agree   SD = Strongly Disagree
 A = Agree   D = Disagree

_____ 1. I think that anger is a normal emotion which all people experience.

_____ 2. I think that our society as a whole does not do a good job of helping people deal with their anger.

_____ 3. I think that heart attacks and other physical problems may be the result of persons not handling their anger in constructive ways.

_____ 4. I can remember at least one time that I was physically sick because I was so angry about something.

_____ 5. If children are too often forced to repress their angry or hostile tendencies, they may end up unable to stand up for their own rights.

_____ 6. I would rather give in to the wishes of another person than become involved in a heated exchange of words.

_____ 7. Children who are angry at their parents should be given opportunity to express that anger directly to their parents.

_____ 8. Children who are angry at their teacher(s) should be given opportunity to express that anger directly to their teacher(s).

_____ 9. Most children have considerable power over their parents.

_____10. Adults who feel powerless or insecure in their own being are the ones who are most likely to abuse their children.

_____11. Some infants, from the time of birth, act in such a way that their parents are more likely to abuse them than to abuse other children in the same family.

_____12. I have been angry enough to want to do serious physical harm to another person.

_____13. I have been angry enough to want to hit another person.

_____14. I have been angry enough to hit another person (since the time I was in elementary school).

_____15. I think that most teachers are not sufficiently aware of the power which they have over the children whom they instruct.

_____16. I think that society as a whole does a better job protecting the rights of parents than the rights of children.

_____17. I think that physical punishment of children is wrong.

_____18. I think that fraternity and sorority activities like hazings and initiations, if done with reasonable care, may provide a healthy outlet for normal aggressiveness.

_____19. God did not give us enough wisdom to properly handle anger.

_____20. A Christian should learn how to deal with anger in a way that avoids hurting others.

ACTIVITY #3: Go through today's newspaper. Find as many examples as you can of both proper and improper handling of angry feelings. You may wish to make a collage by using glue to mount words, articles, and pictures on newsprint or posterboard. If you are working with a group, these can be used as the basis for further discussion.

ACTIVITY #4: Look again at the discussion of ANGER, ASSERTIVE-NESS, AND AGGRESSION. If you are in a group, you might enjoy acting out the situations which are described in the text. (Don't get TOO explicit in the scene involving Kim and Tom!) What other options besides those listed in this book may also exist? What situations have you experienced which were similar to those described in the chapter?

ACTIVITY #5: During the coming week, keep a personal record of the times when you feel angry. What causes your anger? How do you feel about the manner in which you handled your anger? What improvements would you like to make in the way that you handle anger?

CHAPTER TWO

HANDLING ANGER

- Bob couldn't remember his hallway conversation with the principal. It was like he had tuned out everything that the man had said. Bob had been so angry that all his effort had gone into self-control. He knew that he should have responded to the charges the principal made. But he couldn't. If he had tried to talk, he would have exploded. He would have yelled or screamed or worse.

- Martha yelled at her mother: "Leave me alone! Leave me alone! I can't take any more pressure. I can't do any better. I don't want to talk about it. I just want to be alone."

- Tom had thought he would impress Sarah by getting her car started for her. But it didn't work out that way. He couldn't jump her car, because his car wouldn't start. He got out, jerked open the hood of the car, but could find nothing wrong. It should have started. The discount store had to have sold him a piece of junk; the battery was no good. He looked across the parking lot. He could see Sarah waiting inside her car. Now he felt stupid. He kicked the front of his car. Then it was worse. The old metal of the grill gave way and jabbed into the radiator. Tom wanted to die.

- Sam had not cheated on the test. Mrs. Walker had no right to accuse him. He had studied hard, and he knew the information. He could have been doing good work all along, but he just hadn't been motivated. He wanted to hit her. He wanted to run away. He wanted to do anything but sit there and listen to her gravelly voice. He couldn't take it. He threw the books on the floor and ran out of the room. It sounded like Walker was throwing pieces of gravel after him.

- Beth missed two days of school. She couldn't keep food down. She kept throwing things up. The doctor didn't think she had the flu. She lacked the other symptoms. Her mother kept asking her if anything was wrong at school, and Beth insisted that there was not. But all Beth could think about was Ed. He had left her. He had really left her. What was he doing with Janice? Were they sleeping together? He had slept with Beth quick enough. Why had he left her? Why had he started going out with Janice? Why hadn't he said anything to her? Other people told her that he was going out with Janice. But she hadn't believed it. He'd just told her that he was busy with homework and wouldn't be seeing as much of her. He sure wasn't seeing much of her. He wasn't seeing any of her. Beth hoped something was wrong with her appendix or that she had some rare tropical disease. She didn't want to be sick because she was so hurt and angry with Ed.

How should you handle anger? There are lots of options. And what's best in one situation may not be what's best in another. Whom you're angry with and what you're angry about have an impact on the response you should choose. Your own personality is also an important factor. What works well for one person may not work well for another. The concepts which follow may help you in decision making.

YELL, RUN, OR THROW SOMETHING

Lot's of people have learned to cope with anger by yelling, running, or throwing something. Doing that can relieve the initial tension, but this approach is almost always a problem if done in front of other people. In fact, others may be so angry with you for being angry that they'll miss the reason for the anger!

If yelled or screamed at, most of us go on the defensive. We feel threatened and insecure. When we yell at others, we cause those same responses.

Ralph's mother had done it again. She wouldn't lay off of him. Not even for a few minutes. He stormed out the door and slammed it hard behind him. He wasn't going to take any more off of her.

SLAM

OUTA MY WAY, ☆?℅⚡!

We've all felt that way and have all wanted to respond that way. But we also know what happens when we give into the initial impulse to yell or hit or run. Others get madder at us, and we inevitably feel foolish later. When working with other people, there are very few occasions when an initially hostile response is the best one.

That DOESN'T mean that you should never yell or hit something. Yelling can be an excellent release of angry feelings, and it can be of great value. What's important is to choose carefully the place from which you yell. The best option is normally to yell in the privacy of your own home or some other place where people will not hear you. If you're going to yell at home to release your tension, warn any others who are home. Otherwise they'll think you've lost your mind or are angry with them. If you are angry with someone at home, then it's best to find another place to scream. Use the home of a friend or an open field or the inside of a car.

Hitting can also be helpful—but don't hit another person or kick a cat or break a lamp or smash a car. Use a punching bag or hit a pillow or kick the side of a sturdy tree. This helps release physical tension without hurting anyone.

REMEMBER—yelling and screaming and hitting and kicking are good methods for blowing off tension and anger in private. But they are HORRI-BLE methods for communicating with other people. If you yell at someone or hit someone, the recipient of your violence will only remember the violence—and not the issue which caused your angry response.

Running away from a situation generally is not a good idea. You usually offend the other person and end up not getting all the information which you need. There are, however, EXCEPTIONS. If you are so angry that you genuinely feel that you can't control yourself, then it may be best to ask for a postponement of the discussion. Try not to say a great deal, but make it clear that you are not prepared to deal with the subject yet. NEVER leave the scene of a heated encounter without explaining your departure and sharing your intention to continue the discussion at another time.

BATACAS, BOOKS, AND PILLOWS

Picking something to throw or hit isn't always easy. Some sporting goods stores carry special foam rubber bats called batacas. They make a good swish and a loud impact, but they are not normally harmful to yourself or others. We'll say more about batacas later in the book. Pillows work very well. Hitting a mattress can also be good.

Some people find a lot of release in throwing a paperback book. If you don't care about keeping the book in good condition and are careful where you throw it, this can be all right.

A punching bag and gloves can help. You can pound on an old board with a hammer, if there is workshop space in your basement or garage.

Remember, however, that the purpose of throwing or hitting anything is that of ventilating your own anger and frustration—not that of hurting anyone.

> **NEVER DRIVE A CAR IF YOU ARE TOO ANGRY TO MAINTAIN CONTROL.**

PHYSICAL EXERCISE

Hard physical exertion can be an excellent means of ventilating hostility. While a punching bag can certainly provide that, you can also find release in:

- Taking a long walk
- Having a hard run
- Swimming
- Playing a game of exertion like basketball
- Riding a bicycle
- Jumping a rope

Or any other kind of physical exercise which you enjoy.

CLEAR THINKING

> **"Be careful how you think; your life is shaped by your thoughts."**
>
> —Proverbs 4:23 (TEV)

LOTS of our problems with handling anger are the result of unrealistic expectations about life. When you take time to think about the person, incident, or situation which has caused your anger, you may begin to see things differently.

Think about the statements which follow. Serious examination shows that the statements are false, but many of us react to life as though the statements were true.

FALSE STATEMENT #1: You should be loved by everyone. Of course, it would be nice to be loved by everyone—or at least to be liked by everyone. But life isn't like that. No matter what you do; no matter what you say; no matter where you live—you will not be loved by everyone. The personality characteristics that make you liked by some will make you disliked by others. Yet many of us act as though it should be possible to be loved by everyone, and we react with anger when others do not give us the affection which we feel we deserve.

We either respond by being angry at those who fail to give us the affection which (we think) we deserve; or we are mad at ourselves for not behaving in such a way that others will love us.

NOW—you should be loved by some people, and you should be liked by many others. If NO ONE loves you, you certainly have reason to be concerned. But the fact that everyone does not love you does not mean that something is wrong with other people or with yourself.

In fact, too great a desire to be liked by others can be dangerous. Bill had spent most of his life confined to a wheelchair. Steve had been one of his closest friends and greatly enjoyed being with him. But Bill had a serious problem with control of his bladder and intestines. He also perspired a great deal. The result was that Bill always smelled. It was a smell which others could endure when they were familiar with it, but it was a source of rude jokes by many who did not know Bill well. Steve was with a group of people when they began making jokes about Bill and talking about how they couldn't stand to be near him. Steve knew that he should have spoken up on Bill's behalf, but he very much wanted the friendship of the others. So he kept quiet. Then he discovered that Bill had heard the conversation, and it was one of the worst days of Steve's life.

You won't be liked by everyone. You can't be liked by everyone. Trying too hard to do so will have you changing masks frequently. Be yourself. MOST will like you as you are. Plastic people are disliked by themselves and by others.

MASKS OF LIFE

Plastic people,
Speak to me
Of truth and beauty and
Honesty.
I tried to touch reality
With the plastic people
Known to me,
But they laughed and they lied
As they ran far away —
For they can't admit the truth
In the light of the day.

—Miriam Messerly

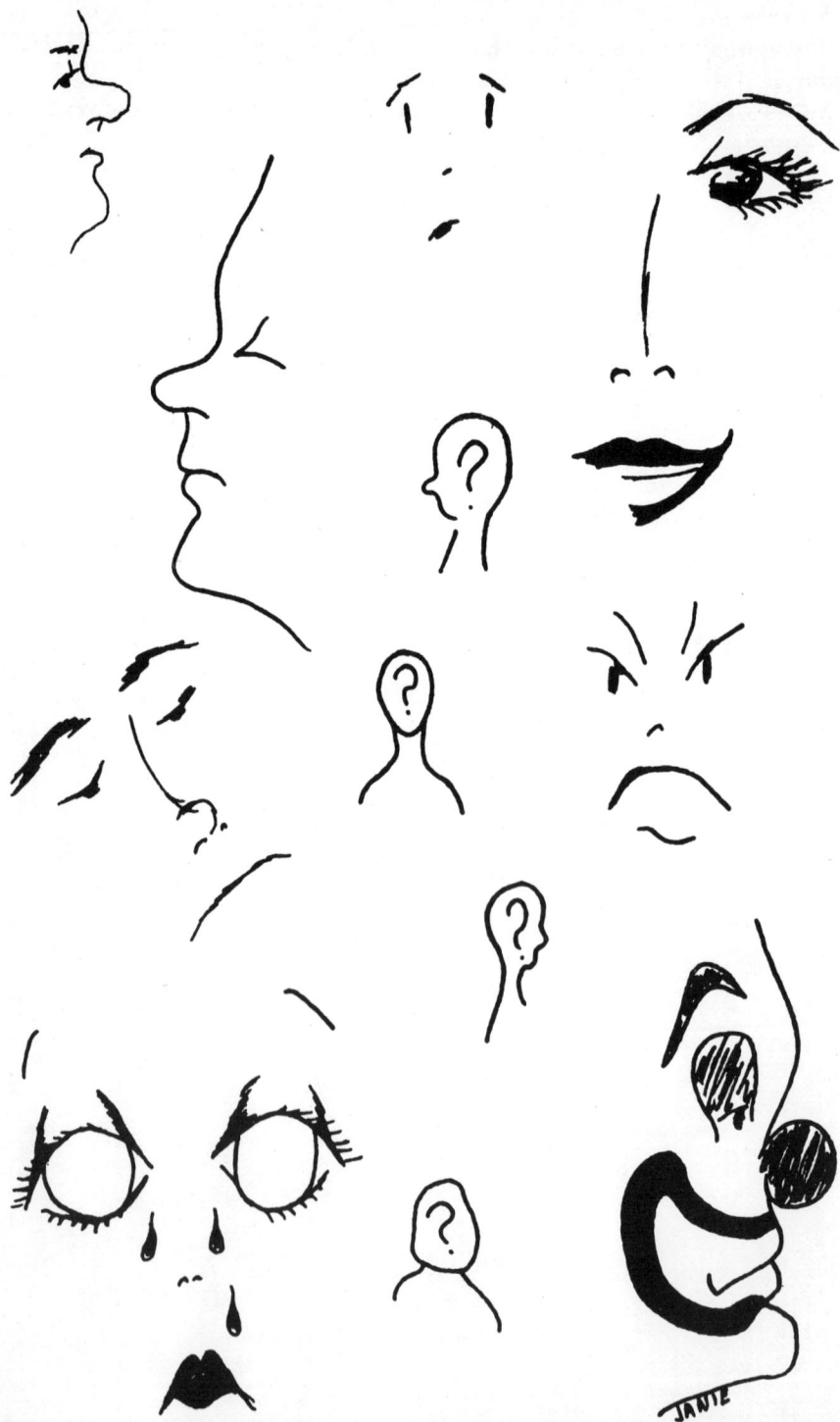

FALSE STATEMENT #2: You should be able to avoid making any mistakes. We all know that this statement is false, but we often judge ourselves and others as though it was true. Imperfection is part of our human lot. That's true for you; and that's true for your friends, family, teachers, and acquaintances. You and others will:

- Forget birthdays
- Dent car fenders
- Yell at others
- Turn in messy homework
- Oversleep
- Overeat
- Drop things
- Trip over things
- Walk into other people
- Space out and lose track of a conversation
- Misunderstand what someone else said
- Put off an important phone call

And so the list could be continued! Obviously you should be concerned if you keep denting fenders or if oversleeping becomes a daily event or if spacing out in the middle of conversations becomes a pattern. But all of us will show those and countless other aggravating, annoying, and plain stupid behaviors. You need to be patient with yourself and also be patient with others. In Biblical terms, that means being willing to forgive yourself and others. Peter inquired of Jesus how much forgiveness had to be extended to others:

> **Then Peter came up and said to him, "Lord, how often shall my brother sin against me, and I forgive him? As many as seven times?" Jesus said to him, "I do not say to you seven times, but seventy times seven."**
>
> **—Matthew 18:21-22 (RSV)**

Those of us who fail to accept the reality of human error will go through life angry at ourselves and angry at others. Forgiveness, sometimes on a daily basis, must be a basic part of all healthy human relationships. And you should be patient with yourself as well as with others.

FALSE STATEMENT #3: When things are bad, they will never get better. Again, the statement is obviously false. But when we are miserable or hurt or angry, we generally respond as though there is no hope—as though the unhappiness or pain or rage of the moment will continue through all eternity. But we know that is false. Things do change. Sometimes change comes in a matter of minutes. Sometimes change comes in a matter of years. And sometimes change does not come in the manner expected or desired. But change is part of life; every cell in your body is changing every moment of life. The people around you and the world in which you live are also changing.

- The fact that you are lonely now does not mean that you will always be lonely. You may, however, have to reach out to others rather than just waiting on others to reach out to you.
- The fact that you are overweight (or undertall!) or have zits or have small breasts or have generally been a slow developer physically does not mean that your current appearance will hold for the rest of your life. Improve what you can; be patient with the rest.
- The fact that you have been treated unfairly by a teacher does not mean that your educational career is ruined or that you will never achieve in school or that every other teacher will also be unfair.
- The fact that someone you thought was a friend betrayed your friendship does not mean that you will never have a friend who is faithful— and it does not mean that the friend who betrayed you may not become a better friend at a future time.
- The fact that you failed to do your best in a class or in an athletic event or in anything else does not mean that you can't begin doing your best and improving the quality of your life.

Some changes come automatically; some take a great deal of effort on our own part. But change does come.

FALSE STATEMENT #4: Life should be fair. Perhaps life SHOULD be fair—but it isn't. We all know that it isn't. Certainly life was not fair to Christ. Christ's earthly existence ended in death on a cross, betrayed by many who had followed him.

This is a hard fact to accept. We desperately want life to be fair, and something in us DEMANDS that life be fair. But it doesn't work out that way. Part of the problem is that many of us differ on what it would mean for life to be fair. You may desperately want a particular honor or recognition; you may have it coming. But many others may feel exactly the same way. Someone will gain the recognition; someone else will not. In some situations, it is impossible for everyone to come out feeling that things have been fairly determined.

At times life really is unfair. At other times life only seems to be unfair. In any event, we are doomed to go through life angry and frustrated if we insist that things always be fair. EXPECT some disappointment in life. None of us like it, but that's the way it is.

FALSE STATEMENT #5: You should receive appreciation for everything you do for someone else. This seems like a reasonable expectation, but it isn't. Others will not always appreciate what we do for them. There may even be times when the best way to help another person is to do so in secret. Jesus talks about the merits of giving gifts without seeking recognition. Life becomes more enjoyable when we learn to give without expecting repayment in appreciation or in a similar gift or favor. Obviously we enjoy receiving the appreciation of another person; but we should not be too upset when we do not receive that appreciation. After all, a gift or a favor isn't really a gift or favor if we are expecting something in return.

FALSE STATEMENT #6: All rules and laws are unfair and are intended to make you unhappy. Certainly there are rules and laws which are unfair. There are also rules and laws which many of us dislike. But that doesn't mean that ALL rules and laws are unfair. Our country and society as a whole as well as institutions like the school and family could not survive without some laws and rules concerning such things as:

- The protection of the health and welfare of all people.
- The provision of commonly understood laws regulating the flow of traffic. (Think what it would be like to drive if people could go or come as they wished at traffic lights and if people could drive on any side of the road that they wished!)
- The right of children to live free from abuse and to have their basic needs provided.
- Rules and expectations at school, at work, and in the home which are commonly understood.

Clearly there are laws and rules which are unnecessary, and there are many variations in the fairness with which laws and rules are enforced. But some laws and rules are necessary, and laws and rules are generally not directed at any one individual. When we react as though they were, we are not behaving in a rational way.

FALSE STATEMENT #7: Anyone who criticizes you dislikes you. Not so! In fact, sometimes we are criticized the most by those who care about us the most. Criticism is not always the best way to show concern, but it is the only way that some people know. And some criticism is necessary. A teacher who keeps pushing you to do better work in school may be pushing you because he or she sees that you have a great deal of potential and wants you to succeed in school and in a career. Friends who point out changes which you should make in your appearance or attitude generally make those suggestions because they LIKE you. If they didn't like you, they wouldn't care enough to make the suggestions.

If someone continually criticizes you and comes down on you hard, then you may need to talk with that person. But the fact that another person is critical of you does not mean that you are disliked—it often means precisely the opposite!

TALK ABOUT THE PROBLEM

Although there are exceptions, anger is usually best handled by talking about the source of the anger with another person. Try to talk in a soft, non-threatening way if you are discussing your anger with the person whose behavior has prompted it. A soft, calm voice makes it easier to focus on the problem itself.

If your anger is primarily directed at yourself or is about an issue that involves a large number of people, then you should talk about it with a parent, a friend, or an adult who understands you well and will be sympathetic to you. Such a person, however, will also serve you best if willing to point out places at which your own expectations may be wrong.

Although there are a few exceptions, if your anger is directed at a specific person, you generally need to talk with that person. It may be helpful to talk first with someone else just to be sure your understanding of the situation is correct, but you eventually need to talk with the person whose behavior caused your anger. The following kinds of situations happen too often:

- Betty was hurt and angry when her best friend Mary began going out with a fellow on whom Betty had felt she had a claim. Betty was sure that Mary had deliberately taken Matt away from her. As a result, Betty avoided contact with Mary; gave her short, pointed answers to questions; and insisted that "nothing was wrong" when Mary asked why Betty was avoiding her. The truth of the situation was that Matt had enjoyed going out with Betty but felt they were getting too serious. Instead of talking with Betty about it, he just began asking Mary out. Mary declined the first couple of times; but Matt kept asking, so she finally agreed. Mary knew that she should have talked with Betty but felt awkward about doing so. Then Betty showed increasing irritability, and Mary felt less inclined to push the matter in conversation. Several kinds of communication should have taken place.

Matt: certainly should have talked with Betty about his fear that they were getting too serious. He certainly should have done so before asking Mary out.

Mary: should have talked with Betty about Matt's interest before the first time she went out with Matt.

Betty: should have talked with Mary rather than simply assuming that Mary had deliberately taken Matt away.

- Ann knew that her father had been short tempered at home for about three months. Her mother told her that there were some problems at work but that Ann should not worry about it. Ann continued to be concerned but did not know of anything she could do. She was not, however, prepared for her father's angry reaction when she asked about money for a new dress for a dance. Her father yelled at her: "You know that I can't afford a new dress. I can barely afford to make the car payments and the house payments and all the other payments that I have to make to take care of you and the rest of this family. I can't believe you have the nerve to ask for money. If you want money, you get a job." Ann choked back the tears until she was in her own room. Then the hurt changed to anger. Her father had no right to talk with her that way. She hadn't demanded the dress. No one had ever asked her to get a job. In fact, her parents had discouraged her from accepting a job over the summer. They thought it was better for her to enjoy the summer months. Her father apologized briefly at breakfast the next morning and said that she could have money for the dress. Ann accepted the apology but said that she wasn't sure she was going to the dance anyway. She avoided contact with her father and refused to talk about it with her mother. Her mother had not heard the conversation and did not understand why Ann was avoiding her father. Ann's father had absorbed a major pay cut and was in danger of losing his job. But Ann did not know that, and her parents did not tell her. She would have understood the seriousness of the situation if they had told her. Within a few days, her father, who was preoccupied with concern about his job, thought Ann's lack of willingness to do anything with the family was because of something at school or a personal problem. He had forgotten about his angry outburst and did not know that it still was a problem for Ann. Again, several kinds of communication should have taken place:

Ann's parents: should have shared with her the seriousness of their financial situation. If Ann really needed to take a job, they should have talked with her about it.

Ann: probably was not able to talk rationally with her father at the time he exploded at her. She needed time to collect herself, and he needed time to calm down. But she should have spoken with him within a day or two. She needed to tell him how much his outburst had upset her, and she needed to find out what was bothering him so much.

FORGET IT

Most of us do not have the time or emotional energy to respond to everything in life which upsets us. It is probably not worth confronting every rude clerk, unfair teacher, or unpleasant person whom we encounter. It is probably not worth having a lengthy discussion every time a friend or loved one says or does something that hurts us. You should forget what has happened and forge ahead when:

- You are not going to be having any on-going contact with the person or situation which upset you.
- You know, after careful assessment, that there is nothing you can do about the situation and that talking about it with the person or persons involved will only frustrate you.
- You know that your anger was really the result of your own unrealistic expectations or faulty thinking rather than the actions of someone else.
- You can satisfactorily deal with your anger by yelling in the privacy or your own room; through physical exercise; or through a few words of conversation with a friend.

ASSERTIVENESS

You may wish to review again the section in the last chapter which talked about ANGER, AGGRESSION, AND ASSERTIVENESS. Most of us are unable to talk comfortably with those who have displeased us unless we have developed some skill in being assertive—rather than being withdrawn or being aggressive. To be assertive in dealing with another person:

- Talk about the problem rather than making any attack on the worth of the person.
- Acknowledge any responsibility you may have for the problem.
- Show that you understand (if you do!) something of why the other person has acted as she or he has.
- Keep your voice calm and soft so that you are in control of conversation rather than letting your emotions run away with your mouth!
- Ask questions as necessary to be certain you understand the other person's point of view.
- Express appreciation for the other person's willingness to deal with the situation.
- Remember that the other person is a child of God, is loved by God, and should be treated with respect.
- Remember that you are also a child of God and are also entitled to respect.

JOURNALS

Many people find it helpful to keep a daily journal or a weekly journal in which the thoughts, ideas, concerns, and events of life are recorded. The process of writing about things which upset, hurt, anger, or disappoint us can be very helpful. The act of writing down feelings and events often clarifies what has happened and helps us feel better about it.

Some people use the technique of writing a letter in which anger is ventilated—but then tearing up the letter rather than actually sending it. The act of writing down the feelings provides a helpful release. BE SURE not to mail such letters!

PRAYERS

Taking concerns to God in prayer is always appropriate. In fact, the establishment of a regular pattern of personal devotions may do more to help one deal with disappointment, anger, and the problems of life than any other single approach. One should NOT just pray about things that have gone wrong. Prayer should include thanksgiving and a request for God's forgiveness as well as the sharing of problems with God.

The act of prayer often helps us increase our understanding of ourselves, of other people, and of God. God's response to us may come in many ways—through helping us gain new perspectives on a problem, through helping us find the courage to talk with someone about a problem, or through helping us improve our relationship with another person.

Prayer will be of most help in dealing with anger if prayer is a regular part of our lives rather than an act which is simply reserved for emergency situations. A crisis may be a good motivator for the beginning of a devotional pattern, but the pattern should be continued when the crisis has passed.

> **The final portion of this book contains suggestions for devotions and journal writing.**

PROVERBS ON
ANGER AND RELATIONSHIPS

The Old Testament Book of Proverbs contains many helpful sayings on dealing with anger in particular and with human relationships in general. The following verses are all taken from the Today's English Version:

PROVERBS 3:30. "Don't argue with someone for no reason, when he has never done you any harm."

PROVERBS 9:7. "If you correct a conceited man, you will only be insulted. If you reprimand an evil man, you will only get hurt."

PROVERBS 12:1. "A man who loves knowledge wants to be told when he is wrong. It is stupid to hate being corrected."

PROVERBS 12:18. "Thoughtless words can wound as deeply as any sword, but the words of a wise man can heal."

PROVERBS 13:16. "A sensible man always thinks before he acts, but a stupid man advertises his ignorance."

PROVERBS 14:17. "A man with a hot temper does foolish things; a wiser man remains calm."

PROVERBS 15:1. "A gentle answer quiets anger, but a harsh one stirs it up."

PROVERBS 15:28. "Good men think before they answer. Evil men have a quick reply but it causes trouble."

PROVERBS 17:9. "If you want people to like you, forgive them when they wrong you. Remembering wrongs can break up a friendship."

PROVERBS 17:14. "The start of an argument is like the first break in a dam; stop it before it goes any further."

PROVERBS 19:3. "Some people ruin themselves by their own stupid actions, and then blame the Lord."

PROVERBS 20:3. "Any fool can start arguments; the honorable thing is to stay out of them."

PROVERBS 25:21-22. "If your enemy is hungry, feed him; if he is thirsty, give him a drink. You will make him burn with shame, and the Lord will reward you."

PROVERBS 26:2. "Curses cannot hurt you unless you deserve them. They are like birds that fly by and never light."

PROVERBS 27:22. "Even if you beat a fool half to death, he will still be as foolish as ever."

FOR YOU TO DO

ACTIVITY #1: Study carefully the Proverbs in the box PROVERBS ON ANGER AND RELATIONSHIPS. Then read through the following situations. Write in the blank the number of a Proverb which could be applied in each situation. You may find more than one which apply in some instances.

SITUATION A: _____ Pete kept putting off his term paper. He had known about the due date for six weeks, but he kept finding a new excuse to avoid doing it. He stayed up all night before the final deadline, but he was not able to finish the paper. He prayed to God for help and asked God to persuade the teacher to give him another week. Pete approached the teacher then and asked for an extension of time. The teacher told Pete that he was not giving any extensions of time and that Pete would fail the paper. Pete feels like God let him down.

SITUATION B: _____ Bill was walking down the school hallway when Fred grabbed him by the arm and pushed him against the wall. Fred was so angry that he almost spat the words out of his mouth: "I heard what you were saying about me to Tammy. You had no right to do that. I don't drink any more than you do, and that car accident wasn't my fault. You just don't want her going out with me. You want her for yourself. Right?"

   Bill was conscious that several people were listening to them, but he forced himself to speak in a low voice: "I'm sorry you feel that way. I don't know what you heard that I said to her. I want to talk with you more about it but not in the middle of the hallway between classes. I'll buy you a coke after school."

SITUATION C: _____ When Mrs. Rogers finished going over Miriam's paper with her, she was surprised by Miriam's saying: "Thanks for taking the time to go over this. It bothered me when you called me in, because I knew I should have done better on the paper. But you've really helped me understand how I can improve, and I'll try to do better."

SITUATION D: _____ Sarah refused to get involved in a nasty political discussion with two others at her table in the cafeteria. She later explained her logic to a friend: "I disagreed strongly with what they said, but I couldn't see anything to gain from getting involved in the argument. I don't know them well enough for them to accept my views without getting mad. And I didn't see any way that I would change their minds."

If you are discussing these materials in a group setting, be sure to talk about your responses to the preceeding items. How do you feel about the way each situation was handled? Should anything have been done differently?

ACTIVITY #2: Review again the materials on assertiveness in this chapter and in the last chapter. Then think about how you would handle each of the following situations. If you are in a class or group, you may wish to role play or act out these situations:

A. You need to tell your father/mother/boyfriend/girlfriend/husband/ wife that you have put a big dent in his or her car.
B. You need to tell your waiter or waitress that your steak is not prepared as you had requested it.
C. You need to tell a teacher that you feel you are being treated unfairly.
D. You need to tell an employer that you believe a policy is unfair.
E. You need to confront a close friend who keeps making slams on members of another race.
F. You need to tell your minister that a lot of people are unhappy with the way in which he or she is preaching.
G. You need to get a mechanic to correct a previous error in servicing your car.

ACTIVITY #3: How do you feel about the law and authority? Respond to the following statements using these symbols:

SA = Strongly Agree   SD = Strongly Disagree
A = Agree   D = Disagree

Compare your responses with those of others, if possible.

_____ 1. Most of the rules in my school are fair and are needed.
_____ 2. I expect teachers to enforce school rules and do not resent their actions in doing so.
_____ 3. Most of the rules and expectations my parents have for me are fair and are needed.
_____ 4. I expect my parents to enforce the rules that have been set for me and do not resent their actions in doing so.
_____ 5. Most of the laws that police officers are expected to enforce are fair and are needed.
_____ 6. I expect police officers to enforce the law and do not resent their actions in doing so.
_____ 7. I feel I should have a greater role in setting rules at school.
_____ 8. I feel I should have a greater role in setting the rules and expectations my parents have of me.
_____ 9. I feel young people should have a greater voice in determining public laws that affect them.
_____ 10. I know what my legal rights are if I should be arrested.
_____ 11. Present laws adequately protect the rights of young persons.
_____ 12. Present laws about marijuana usage are fair and needed.

_____ 13. Present laws about drinking age and punishment for underage drinking are fair and needed.

_____ 14. Curfew laws are a needed control on the behavior of many young people.

_____ 15. CB radios should be made illegal because so many people use them to avoid arrest for traffic violations.

_____ 16. I feel that many police officers enjoy having authority and power over others.

_____ 17. I would personally enjoy having the authority that police officers are given.

_____ 18. In general, most young people need to be given more responsibility and freedom.

_____ 19. Police officers are more concerned with curfew and traffic violations than with solving major crimes such as murder and armed robbery.

_____ 20. Legal cases involving teen-age offenders should be handled by a different court system than those involving adult offenders.

_____ 21. Many police officers do not extend the same courtesy to teen-age suspects as to adult suspects.

_____ 22. Law enforcement agencies should not keep records on crimes committed by teen-agers or at least should destroy those records after a certain period of time.

_____ 23. The high rate of traffic accidents involving teen-agers gives good support to arguments for raising the age for obtaining a driver's license.

_____ 24. Most young people distrust police officers.

If you are with a class or group, you may wish to invite a police officer or a school principal to visit with your group about laws and rules which seem unfair and which may provoke angry reactions from teenagers and others.

ACTIVITY #4: This chapter has included several approaches to dealing with anger. The response which is best depends on the other person (or persons) involved, on the situation, and on your own personality. Review the following list of approaches, and look back at the text of the chapter if you need more information. Then read the situations which follow. Decide on the general approach which would be best for you personally in dealing with each situation. If possible, share your responses with others. You may find it helpful to act out or role play some of the situations.

> **Approaches to Handling Anger**
>
> Yell, Run, or Throw Something
> Batacas, Books, and Pillows
> Physical Exercise
> Clear Thinking
> Talk About the Problem
> Forget It
> Assertiveness
> Journal
> Prayer

Situations

In many instances, you may wish to use a combination of approaches. If so, think about the order in which you would want to use the approaches. (For example, clear thinking followed by talking about the problem followed by prayer.)

1. Your best friend has forgotten your birthday.
2. A clerk in a store has given you $5 too little change.
3. Your brother has borrowed a book from you without permission.
4. Your grandmother has complained about the way you wear your hair.
5. Two strangers sitting in front of you during a movie are making so much noise that you have trouble hearing the film.
6. Your minister parked too close to your car, and you think his car took a little paint from the side of your car.
7. You have trouble doing somersaults in physical education, and you are angry because two of your friends keep making fun of you.
8. A friend keeps asking to copy your homework, and you feel increasingly angry over his not doing the work himself.
9. You are angry with yourself for doing poorly on a test.
10. You are upset because your mother keeps snapping at you about homework, housework, and life in general.

ACTIVITY #5: Have a pillow fight or a bataca fight with some other people. Think about some of the things that have frustrated you during the past week before beginning the pillow or bataca fight. Ten minutes is probably a long enough duration for the fight! Then talk about how you feel following the fight. In what ways could you obtain the same benefit from some other form of physical exercise? Would the activity have been more helpful if you had been mad about something that had happened shortly before the fight? Why, or why not?

CHAPTER THREE

ANGER AT YOURSELF

I HATE MYSELF!

I WISH I COULD DIE!

WHY DID I DO THAT?

LIFE STINKS!

I FEEL LIKE CRUD!

God made rivers;
God made lakes;
God made me;
But we all make mistakes!

I FEEL LIKE A PIG!

Unless you are abnormal, you have times when you can strongly identify with one or more of the above statements. Most of us have times at which we are not happy with ourselves and may in fact hate ourselves more than anyone else in the world. Check each category which represents something for which you have been angry at yourself:

_____ Failing a test.

_____ Being fired from a job.

_____ Losing your temper with a member of your family.

_____ Losing your temper with a friend.

_____ Losing your temper with a clerk in a store.

_____ Being afraid to say what you think in a group.

_____ Letting someone else take unfair advantage of you.

_____ Manipulating someone into doing what you want.

_____ Lying to someone.

_____ Sharing gossip which is cruel or hurtful.

_____ Not going to church.

_____ Wasting money.

_____ Forgetting the birthday of a friend.

_____ Not having saved enough money.

_____ Overeating.

_____ Not staying on a program of regular exercise.

_____ Wasting time.

_____ Breaking something.

_____ Having a car accident.

_____ Oversleeping.

_____ Hitting another person.

_____ Being jealous of another person.

_____ Wanting revenge on another person.

_____ Not praying on a regular basis.

_____ Being insensitive to the needs of other people.

The list can be continued! Most of us can do an excellent job identifying our own shortcomings, and self analysis often results in self hatred.

THE TROUBLE WITH HATING YOURSELF

None of us WANT to hate ourselves. It is important to recognize some of the consequences of excessive anger at ourselves.

First, anger which is turned inward can cause physical problems. Severe headaches, high blood pressure, asthma, upset stomach, ulcers, backache, and other physical symptoms can result from being excessively angry at ourselves. In fact, if you are plagued with repeated physical symptoms which have not been satisfactorily explained in other ways, you may need to consider the possibility that those symptoms are the result of emotional problems. The physical symptoms, of course, are just as unpleasant and just as serious as if they were the result of physical injury or infection.

Second, it's hard to get along with others when you're mad at yourself. The Biblical admonition to "love others as you love yourself" or to "do unto others as you would have them do unto you" does not work well if you hate yourself or would like to hurt yourself. It's extremely difficult to be sensitive to the needs of other people when you're filled with self-hatred.

Third, it's hard to work at your best when you are filled with self-hatred. Most of us can only concentrate on one thing at a time. If you can't push your thoughts about yourself from the center of your mind, you will find it difficult to concentrate on any task.

Fourth, self-hatred sometimes leads to suicide. In the United States and Canada, suicide is the second highest killer of people between the ages of ten and twenty-four. Only automobile accidents claim more lives. It is tragic when one attempts to destroy the life which God has given.

Fifth, self-hatred may keep us from being open to God's love. Indeed, if we repeatedly hate ourselves, that hatred comes about at least in part because we have not been fully open to God's love. We are not accidents, and we are certainly not (as the short poem at the start of the chapter mistakenly says) mistakes. Even so-called unwanted children who come as a result of unexpected pregnancies are wanted and loved by God. The Scriptures repeatedly emphasize the centrality of God's love for us and of God's desire for our lives to be meaningful and good. When we hate ourselves, it is difficult to be open and receptive to God's love.

GOD'S LOVE FOR US

The verses which follow are only a few of those in Scripture which speak of God's great love for us.

JOHN 3:16. "For God so loved the world that he gave his only Son, that whoever believes in him should not perish but have eternal life."

JOHN 15:9. "As the Father has loved me, so have I loved you; abide in my love."

ROMANS 5:8. "But God shows his love for us in that while we were yet sinners Christ died for us."

ROMANS 8:35, 38-39. "Who shall separate us from the love of Christ? Shall tribulation, or distress, or persecution, or famine, or nakedness, or peril, or sword? . . . For I am sure that neither death, nor life, nor angels, nor principalities, nor things present, nor things to come, nor powers, nor height, nor depth, nor anything else in all creation, will be able to separate us from the love of God in Christ Jesus our Lord."

1 JOHN 4:7-8. "Beloved, let us love one another; for love is of God, and he who loves is born of God and knows God. He who does not love does not know God; for God is love."

1 JOHN 4:19. "We love, because he first loved us."

THE ROOTS OF SELF-HATRED

How we see ourselves and how we feel about ourselves depends in large part on experiences of early childhood. The manner in which we were treated by our parents, our brothers and sisters, friends, and other adults has a great deal to do with our self-worth. What were those experiences like?

DID YOU

_____ feel consistently loved and protected as a child?

OR

_____ often feel rejected or unwanted?

DID YOU

_____ learn that mistakes are normal and can be forgiven?

OR

_____ learn that mistakes are horrible and that people who make mistakes are bad?

OR

_____ did your parents overprotect you and fail to point out mistakes to you?

DID YOU

_____ learn a basically positive view of other people and have contact with many people who showed you affection?

OR

_____ learn to be very suspicious of other people and have very little contact with people outside the household?

DID YOU

_____ feel accepted and loved even when your parents found it necessary to punish you for someting?

OR

_____ feel rejected and not loved at all when your parents found it necessary to punish you for something?

DID YOU

_____ have rules, expectations, punishments, and rewards which you were able to understand and which seemed to be consistent?

OR

_____ have rules, expectations, punishments, and rewards which were changed so frequently that you did not know what was expected of you?

DID YOU

_____ learn that God loves you; wants the best for you; is willing to forgive you when you sin; and wants to help you have a meaningful life?

OR

_____ learn that God will judge you; expects perfect obedience from you; will punish you when you sin; and wants you to have a restricted, cautious life?

DID YOU

_____ develop appreciation for your own knowledge, talent, and ability?

OR

_____ remain unsure of your own knowledge, talent, and ability?

OR

_____ develop a feeling of false superiority over people who seem less intelligent or skilled than yourself?

DID YOU

_____ learn that the material possessions and financial wealth of an individual have nothing to do with that person's worth as a child of God?

OR

_____ learn that "you are what you own" and that one's worth depends on possessions and income?

DID YOU

_____ learn that life carries many frustrations, and that one cannot live without sometimes being hurt or disappointed?

OR

_____ learn that life "owes" you the things that you want and that you should be able to get through life without major hurts or disappointments?

In each of the preceding pairs or triads of statements, the first statement represents the view which usually results in the healthiest self-image. It is very important to grow up feeling good about yourself, about the love of others for you, about your own intelligence and ability, and about God's love for you. It is also important to recognize that financial success has nothing to do with success in the eyes of God and that life inevitably brings us some hurts and disappointments.

Very few people will check the first option in every single instance in the DID YOU? list. None of us are perfect, and that includes parents. We included the list for two reasons. First, understanding that some of one's self-hatred or low self-worth is rooted in early childhood experiences can often be helpful in trying to make changes and improvements in one's life. Second, all of us have some contact with small children; most of us will be parents; and we all have opportunities to help children develop positive self-images.

ORDINARY PEOPLE

In the book and movie *ORDINARY PEOPLE*, a teenage boy carries an enormous load of guilt from the drowning accident of his brother. He blames himself for not having prevented the accident and feels (with some good reason) that his mother always preferred his brother to himself. To some extent, both he and his mother act as though the accident was the result of his weakness, though that view is never shown to be an accurate one.

When his one attempt at suicide is unsuccessful, he attempts to bury the anger he feels about the death of his brother, his mother's distant and cold attitude, and his father's seeming inability to help the situation. His depression does not lift until he is finally able to forgive himself and to feel secure in the love of his father.

Thought not all of us will deal with incidents as traumatic as a drowning accident, we will all face the death of loved ones, failure in some relationships, and failure to do our best at school or work. Whether our acceptance of the blame for such losses is rational or irrational (right or wrong; smart or stupid), the ability to accept and forgive ourselves is of great importance.

The title of the book and the movie (which was based on the book) is appropriate—*ORDINARY PEOPLE*. We are all ordinary people. Ordinary people hurt, suffer, make mistakes, cry, hate themselves, hate others, want desperately to be loved, mess up their lives, show courage under surprising circumstances, and find redemption as they feel forgiveness and love.

SELF-AWARENESS
OTHER-AWARENESS

Much of our sense of self-worth depends on how accurately we see ourselves and on how accurately we understand the feelings of others toward us. The first is a matter of SELF-AWARENESS. The second is what might be called OTHER-AWARENESS.

Inaccurate self-awareness and other-awareness can result in considerable anger toward ourselves. Consider these people:

MARCIE hates herself. She's over-weight and can't make herself stay on a diet. She's afraid of members of the opposite sex and doesn't think they would like her even if she were thin. She's a high school junior.

BILL is one of the best students in his high school. His grades are high, but he has not been successful in athletic activities. He feels uncoor-dinated—a real klutz! He's con-vinced that others look at him with disgust or pity because he is not more successful in physical events.

DAN and CINDY have been mar-ried for two years. Cindy has just accepted a new job which involves a great deal of pressure. She is very aware that the last person in her position was fired. She's upset about work when she comes home at the end of the day, but she has not yet felt like telling Dan just how much pressure she feels. Dan sees her as being withdrawn and moody. He feels certain that she must be unhappy with something that he's doing. Even though she has told him that her moodiness is related to her job, he still chooses to believe that she must be angry with him. He thinks she is being unfair and becomes increasingly angry with her.

TED is a sophomore in college. He is majoring in chemistry, but he is disap-pointed with his grades thus far. His best subject seems to be sociology, but he sees few good employment oppor-tunities available to persons with that major. His father is a chemical engineer, and Ted has always wanted to enter a related field. College has been a miserable experience. In many ways he doesn't want to be a chemist, but he feels like changing his major is just running away from a hard situa-tion. Besides that, he knows of no sub-ject except sociology in which he could

be reasonably certain of good grades.
Ted continues to feel stupid in com-
parison to some chemistry majors who
seem to understand the material far
more easily. He doesn't feel likely to
succeed at anything.

ANN is thirty-eight years old. Her
youngest child is in high school, and
she has a child who just entered col-
lege. Ann did not attend college. She
and her husband were married im-
mediately after her high school gradua-
tion, and she helped put him through
college. She now feels somewhat angry
and resentful of the opportunities
which her own children have which
were denied her. Her husband has sug-
gested that she go back to college, but
she doesn't believe that she could do
satisfactory work. Her grades in high
school were excellent, but she doesn't
feel she could keep up today. In many
ways she wishes that she had not gotten
married or had children.

As you can see, the self-awareness and the other-awareness of many people is not completely accurate. The fact that Marcie is overweight does not mean that others do not like her; it also does not mean that males will not like her. She may be afraid of coping with members of the opposite sex; and the fact that she continues to be overweight and therefore (in her opinion) unattractive protects her from dealing with dating situations.

It's very doubtful that others look at Bill with disgust and pity. Lots of people have problems with coordination and skill in athletic events. Bill is hardly alone in that way. Some people may seem to be disgusted with him simply because Bill expects them to respond in that way. He should be thinking much more about his ability in academic classes than about his nonability in athletics.

Cindy obviously needs to have told Dan more about the pressure she feels in her job. At the same time, Dan is being irrational in assuming that the on-ly reason Cindy could be upset is because he has done something that angers or hurts her. He is unable to be supportive of her because he is so busy feel-ing threatened himself. Cindy can't get past her own problems to see the af-fect that her withdrawn behavior has on Dan.

Ted has generalized from the fact that he has trouble with a chemistry major to the conclusion that he cannot do well in any field that is REALLY worth pursuing. He has (without consciously deciding to do so) made success in chemistry the major standard by which he evaluates his life and his possibilities for career success.

Ann is too busy feeling angry about her situation and sorry for herself to recognize that many opportunities are available for her. She no longer has small children at home, and thirty-eight is certainly not too late an age to return to school—especially if her husband is supportive of that goal. If she made good grades before, it is reasonable to assume that she can again make good grades. Her resentment of the opportunities which her own children have may be making it difficult for her to give to them and receive from them needed encouragement and support.

AWARENESS TEST

This test is designed to measure the extent to which you have reasonably accurate awareness of your own strengths and weaknesses and of the people around you. You will need a watch with a second hand or a digital clock that records seconds in order to take this test. Then look at the discussion of your score at the end of the test.

_____ 1. Take exactly thirty seconds. In that thirty seconds, identify TEN characteristics or traits or abilities that you LIKE about yourself. Score yourself one point for each characteristic you identify up to a maximum of ten points.

_____ 2. Take exactly twenty seconds. In that twenty seconds, identify TEN characteristics or traits or abilities that you DISLIKE about yourself. Score yourself one point for each characteristic you identify up to a maximum of ten points.

_____ 3. Think about the classes, groups, and meetings which you have attended during the past week. Has there been an occasion at which you wanted to say something; failed to say something because you were afraid you were wrong; and then discovered that your idea was a good one? If you can think of an occasion, write NO points in the blank. If you cannot think of such an occasion, write a score of FIVE in the blank.

_____ 4. Think about the times in the past week that you have been at stores, shopping centers, the homes of friends, or other places away from your own home or school. Has there been an occasion at which you NEEDED to go to the bathroom but did not do so because you did not feel comfortable asking someone for directions to a bathroom? If you can think of an occasion, write NO points in the blank. If you cannot think of an occasion, write a score of FIVE in the blank.

_____ 5. Do you feel certain of the existence of God and the reality of God's love for your life? If you do not feel certain, write NO points in the blank. If you DO feel certain, write a score of TEN in the blank.

_____ 6. Take exactly ten seconds. Can you immediately recall and describe the clothes that you were wearing two days ago? If you can, write a score of FIVE in the blank. If you cannot, write NO points in the blank.

_____ 7. Take exactly twenty seconds. Can you immediately recall and describe the clothes that your closest friend wore two days ago? If you can, write a score of FIVE in the blank. If you cannot, write NO points in the blank.

_____ 8. Can you identify at least three people who LOVE you a great deal? If you can, write a score of TEN in the blank. If you cannot, write NO points in the blank.

_____ 9. Can you identify at least one person who would be willing to sacrifice his or her own life in order to save your life? If you can, write a score of TEN in the blank. If you cannot, write NO points in the blank.

_____ 10. Can you identify at least three times in the past two days when you have been very angry with yourself? Give yourself TWO points for EACH time that you can identify up to a maximum of six points.

_____ 11. Can you identify at least one time in the past week that you have been so unhappy with yourself that you did not want to be alive? If you can identify such a time, write NO points in the blank. If you cannot identify such a time, write TEN points in the blank.

_____ 12. Take exactly ten seconds. Can you immediately recall what you had for lunch three days ago? If you can, write a score of FIVE in the blank. If you cannot, write NO points in the blank.

_____ 13. Take exactly thirty seconds. Think of your three closest friends (or people you like to be around the most). Identify as many ways as you can in which those three persons are all alike—up to a maximum of five ways. Score yourself two points for each way up to maximum of ten points.

If thirty seconds was not enough, take another thirty seconds to complete the task. Give yourself one point for each way during the last thirty seconds—but you only get points for a maximum of five ways in the total sixty seconds. (SO, suppose you identified two ways in the first thirty seconds and two ways in the second thirty seconds. Then your total score for this item would be four points from the first thirty seconds and two points from the second thirty seconds for a total of six points.)

_____ 14. Take exactly ten seconds. Can you immediately remember the circumstances under which your PARENTS met each other? If you can, write a score of FIVE in the blank. If you cannot, write NO score in the blank. If your parents are not alive or if you have not lived with your parents for the past two years, write a score of FIVE in the blank.

AWARENESS TEST INTERPRETATION

A perfect score would be *101*. Few will achieve that kind of score. An excellent score would be in the 90-101 range. 80-89 would be good; 70-79 would be fair. If your score was below 70, you are NOT a failure; but your awareness may not be as good as it could be. This test has not been standardized against a broad cross section of people, so you shouldn't take your score TOO seriously—but your response to individual items does reveal some things about you.

ITEM #1: Adequate self-awareness includes good knowledge of both your strengths and weaknesses. Thirty seconds is not a lot of time, so you will not be successful at identifying a lot of strengths unless you already have reasonable awareness of the good things about yourself. If you scored low on this one, do a PENANCE of sitting down and listing TWENTY good things about yourself—taking as long as necessary to do it!

ITEM #2: Most of us are more aware of our weaknesses than our strengths. Consequently twenty seconds should be adequate to identify ten things that you dislike about yourself.

ITEM #3: Healthy self-awareness includes the ability to assess whether or not your ideas are good ones. If you consistently fail to express your ideas because you are afraid they will be rejected, you probably do not have adequate awareness of your own insights.

ITEM #4: EVERYONE has to go to the bathroom, and EVERYONE has times when directions to a bathroom are needed. If you feel overly self-conscious about asking for directions to a bathroom, you may not be adequately aware of the extent to which that need is common and such questions are normal.

ITEM #5: For a person struggling to live as a Christian, awareness of God's presence and love are of central importance. Be assured that God DOES love you.

ITEMS 6 & 7: These items may seem as though they measure memory ability. To some extent, this is true. However, not remembering how you and a close friend dressed just two days ago also reflects some lack of attention to yourself and others.

ITEM #8: Unless you are a convicted murderer and live in a prison, there almost certainly are at least three people who love you a great deal. If you are not certain that there are three people who feel that way about you, then you probably do not accurately perceive the feelings of others. If you could not think of three people, try talking with a friend, acquaintance, minister, or another person worthy of trust. Have that person help you assess the extent to which you are adequately aware of the love of others.

ITEM #9: There is almost certainly someone around you who would sacrifice his or her life for your sake. That reality may sound surprising to you. But there are even people who would gladly sacrifice their lives for the sake of a complete stranger—to say nothing of those they know and love. Someone like that IS around you.

ITEM #10: We all have times at which we are angry at ourselves. If you are not aware of such times, then you need to become more sensitive to your own feelings.

ITEM #11: Self-hatred is a normal feeling, but excessive self-hatred harms our relationships with others and our self-awareness. If you hate yourself so much that you frequently wish you were dead, then you probably have a far too negative view of yourself.

ITEM #12: Like items six and seven, this may seem more a matter of memory than of awareness—but the extent to which you know what you have and have not eaten, worn, visited, and so forth does reflect your view of reality.

ITEM #13: Most of us tend to choose friends who share some common characteristics. The more readily you can identify those characteristics, the more likely it is you are aware of the nature of your friends and of what attracts you to them.

ITEM #14: If your parents are not alive or if you have not lived with them for two years, you automatically gain five points on this item. If you are currently living with your parents, however, you should have had enough significant conversation with them to know the circumstances under which they met.

It is almost impossible to directly measure self-awareness and other-awareness. The items used in the AWARENESS TEST are indicators or guides to your awareness—but may not always be accurate reflections.

If you scored low on the test, however, you should recognize the possibility that your self-image and your understanding of other people may not be accurate in some respects.

DEALING WITH ANGER AT YOURSELF

Most of us who have a strong sense of self-contempt have cultivated that feeling over a period of years. Thus there are no quick remedies or easy solutions. The following perspectives and suggestions may be of some worth to you.

First, begin a regular program of Bible study. The devotional suggestions at the end of this book should be of significant help to you. Bible study and prayer help us grow closer to God and make us more aware of God's concern for us and the world.

Second, begin keeping a journal or notebook of your experiences and feelings. The devotional suggestions at the end of the book should help get you started. Discipline yourself to write down the GOOD things you have done as well as the bad, stupid, or bumbling events of your life. Develop skill in recognizing the good that you have done for others.

Third, DO something every day that will make you feel good about yourself. Share a compliment with someone; visit a lonely neighbor; visit a nursing home; write a letter to a friend; make a small donation to a charitable concern; clean a room at the church; . . . The possibilities are endless. But get in the habit of doing things that make you feel good about yourself.

Fourth, take the time to analyze what is happening when you are angry at yourself:

- Should the focus of the anger be at yourself or at someone else? We sometimes focus anger on ourselves when it should actually be directed at another person.

- Have you ACCURATELY interpreted what another person meant? What you are taking for anger or disgust toward yourself from another person may mean something different. It could mean that the other person is actually mad at himself or herself. It could mean that the other person is sick or tired. Don't ASSUME that you are the cause of another person's displeasure unless you are absolutely sure that is true.

- Have you actually done something that different from what hundreds or thousands of other people do every day? The fact that you have made a mistake does not make you a wicked, horrible person. If it does, then the world is filled with wicked, horrible people. Learn to forgive yourself.

Fifth, find someone with whom you can talk about your feelings. Although some people seek a professional counselor for this kind of help, you may find that a friend or relative who cares a great deal about you can give you considerable help. Find someone with whom you can be honest about your feelings of self-hatred, and seek that person's help in looking more realistically at yourself and at the world around you.

FEELING BETTER ABOUT YOURSELF

Do something to help someone else.

Learn to include others.

Find someone you can trust and share your feelings about yourself.

FOR YOU TO DO

ACTIVITY #1: Talk with others about your responses to the check list THE ROOTS OF SELF-HATRED. Do this in a small group or with one other person. Share your responses to the list, and listen to the responses of others. What seem to be some of the most common problems that result in self-hatred? What responsibility do you have to help others form positive self-images?

To what extent, if any, can a bad childhood be seen as an EXCUSE for a person's present behavior? Why can't a person go through life blaming everything on his or her parents and childhood experiences? What can be done to compensate for difficult childhood experiences?

ACTIVITY #2: Look up the verses of Scripture under GOD'S LOVE FOR US. Read the paragraph or section in which those verses are found. What do these verses have to say about the nature of God? What do they say about our worth in God's sight? What do they say about our responsibiities toward other people?

ACTIVITY #3: Read ECCLESIASTES 3:1-13 and MATTHEW 7:24-27. Note that life brings cycles of the good and the bad to all of us. None of us are spared the storms and trials of life. But God is with us through everything that happens. The fact that God loves us does not mean that we are spared having hard times and difficult experiences. What kind of person would you be if you were spared all the trials and hardships of life? According to the passage in Matthew, what can we do to help us in periods of trial? Do we need more to be aware of God's love in the good experiences of life or in the hard experiences of life? Why?

ACTIVITY #4: If you are working with a class or group, have volunteers role play the people described under SELF-AWARENESS/OTHER-AWARENESS. A volunteer should simply take on a role and then describe his or her feelings in that role. Dialogue might begin like this:

MARCIE: "I hate myself. I'm fat. I should be on a diet, but I can't make myself stay with one. I've started several times, but it doesn't work for me. I haven't dated anyone for almost a year. That's not a surprise. Who would go out with a blob like me? . . . "

CINDY: "I don't know how much longer I can stand my job. I have so much trouble keeping up with everything. It's like there's something new to learn every day. You think you're getting on top of it, and then everything falls apart. I know that I should talk more with Dan about it, but I think it would upset him if I did. He means well, but he doesn't do a good job helping me with things like this. . . . "

DAN: "Cindy keeps saying that she isn't mad at me. But I can tell that she is. She wouldn't be acting this way otherwise. I know that I do a lot of things that make her unhappy. I'm slow doing chores around the house. I don't help her enough with work. I'm gone too often in the evening. The problem is that she won't say exactly what it is that upsets her. I know that I'm the problem, but I don't know what to do about it. . . ."

ACTIVITY #5: Take the AWARENESS TEST, and talk about your responses with others. You may not agree with the interpretations put on some of the responses. If you do not, talk about your feelings. Why do you think the test was developed? What concrete things can you do to improve your ability to understand yourself and others?

ACTIVITY #6: If you live in an area which has an emergency telephone counseling service of a public mental health center, see if a volunteer or professional from such an organization can visit with your class or group. Have that person talk about the problem of suicide. You may wish to have that person address:

- Why is suicide such a major problem among the relatively young and the extremely old?
- What relationship exists between self-hatred and suicide?
- What are the signs that someone is considering suicide? What can you do to be of help to someone who feels self-destructive?

ACTIVITY #7: Do this activity with a group of friends you know especially well. It may be with the members of a church class or group, or it may just be with a group of your own friends and acquaintances. Tape a piece of paper on the back of each person. Then give each person a felt-tipped pen or marker. Move around the room, writing notes to each other on the pieces of paper. Write down what you like about each other; how you feel about each other; and what good things you hope happen in the lives of others. When everyone has had time to write on the sheets of several other people, have everyone remove the sheets and take the time to read through them in silence. This is an excellent affirmation exercise and should help you feel better about yourself and about others.

CHAPTER FOUR

ANGER AND POWER

The learner was tightly strapped into the chair. He could not move. He was trying to get the list of nonsense words correct, but it was not an easy task. With each wrong response, he received a jolt of electricity through the chair to which he was strapped. The problem was that each jolt was a little stronger. The theory behind the experiment was that negative reinforcement (PUNISHMENT) can increase the speed of learning but that it takes a minimal level of pain for the speed of learning to actually increase. The shock level was to be gradually increased until the proper or ideal level was found for a particular learner. The shocks were being administered by a paid volunteer who received his instructions from the director of the experiment.

LEARNER: That last shock was pretty strong. I don't think this is working. I'm doing a little worse all the time instead of better. All I can think about is the pain.

DIRECTOR: No need to worry. This is just the design of the experiment. It seems like you aren't learning as rapidly, but you will do better when we reach the right level. It's normal to experience some increased difficulty learning when you are getting close to the right level.

LEARNER: But I'm getting worried. What about my heart? I had some trouble with my heart last year. These shocks are stronger than I'd thought they'd be. I'm not sure that I should continue with this.

DIRECTOR: You have no choice. You agreed to continue with this. We wouldn't set anything up that was actually dangerous. We're scientists here. We're concerned about your welfare. But it isn't possible to stop an experiment in progress. That's part of the contract.

VOLUNTEER: I'm not sure this is a good idea. I wasn't counting on his having a bad heart. We could really hurt him.

DIRECTOR: We've been through this same experiment many times. No one has ever been hurt. No one likes getting shocks, of course. That's why the experiment works. But if you stopped now, all the work would have been wasted. Go on with the next sequence of words.

VOLUNTEER: I want to know what the learner thinks. Do you want the next sequence?

LEARNER:	I don't want to be shocked anymore. You can't keep pushing the voltage up. I don't think I can take it.
DIRECTOR:	That's enough. Get on with it. He's just trying to get your sympathy.
VOLUNTEER:	Sounds to me like he's serious. I'm not turning that voltage up again.
DIRECTOR:	Need I remind you that you as well agreed to the terms of this experiment? We aren't going to stop it for your benefit now. Everything is just fine. You're wasting our time and money.
VOLUNTEER:	All right. Here's the next sequence. . . .

The above script and description are fiction, but the situation is not. Experiments have been done in which volunteers have been asked to shock subjects for the purpose of helping them learn.

THE MILGRAM-ZIMBARDO EXPERIMENTS

The experiments of Stanley Milgram and Philip Zimbardo have special relevance for understanding the relationships of anger, power, and violence in human nature. Stanley Milgram told subjects that they were to help others in a learning experiment by giving those persons mild electric shocks for incorrect responses. Those receiving the shocks were actors, but the subjects were not aware of that. During the course of the experiment, the experimenters urged subjects to increase the intensity of the shocks in order to help the learning process. In spite of the fact that the recipient of the shocks was strapped in a chair and verbalized increasing pain and panic, most subjects continued administering the shocks as long as urged to do so by the experimenter. Had the recipients actually been receiving the shocks, death would have resulted in some cases.

Philip Zimbardo recruited a group of college students who were psychologically screened to eliminate any with unusually hostile or insecure characteristics. They were placed in a simulated prison. Part of the group were made "guards" and the others were made "prisoners." The guards were simply instructed to maintain order and keep the prisoners from escaping. Although the experiment was supposed to have lasted two weeks, Zimbardo terminated it in only six days. Prisoners were starting to show strain, and the guards were becoming increasingly repressive and dehumanizing in their methods of maintaining control.

While the Milgram and the Zimbardo experiments have been the most publicized, other experimenters have conducted similar investigations. The results have been the same: under certain conditions (conditions in no way life threatening to the subjects) ordinary people can be easily motivated to inflict pain or suffering on others. Although we read the history of Nazi Germany and the violent events of daily life with a certain detachment, the reality is that all of us are capable, under some circumstances, of acts of violence which we would normally or theoretically abhor.

Reverse discrimination experiments have become a fairly popular teaching strategy. Though there are many variations, the group is generally divided by some criteria such as "blue eyes" and "brown eyes." One group even receives a favored status and may be permitted to have some power or authority over the other group. In such experiments, roles are usually reversed after a reasonable period of time. The typical object or purpose of the experiment is to help participants better identify with minority groups and to recognize some of the tendencies toward prejudice within themselves.

The first time that we did such an experiment was with a group of teen-agers at a summer camp. The procedure was a simple one and was carefully controlled. The group was told that each person would have two hours to be *master* over someone else and would also experience two hours as the *slave* of that person. The restrictions were adequate: (1) nothing may be required of a slave which carries any danger of physical or psychological damage; (2) slaves may not be required to remove any clothing except shoes and socks; (3) all plans must be written out and approved in advance by a counselor; counselors have absolute veto power; and (4) no one has to participate.

The experience was a good one. Those in the master role required their slaves to do such things as: sing love songs to a water foutain; move objects with their toes; stand tied to a tree; pick up litter from the camp site; and do various exercises and stunts. Before discussing the experience, the 102 participants completed an anonymous questionnaire. Before the experiment began, several had expressed reluctance to be "mean" or "bossy" to another person. After the experience, almost every participant expressed enjoyment, emotional release, or satisfaction from the master role. (Feelings about the slave role were more mixed!)

89 expressed agreement with the statement: "I found it enjoyable to have power over another person."

79 expressed agreement with the statement: "I should have been rougher on my slave."

85 expressed agreement with the statement: "I felt a good emotional release while I was in power."

102 expressed agreement with the statement: "I'm glad that I participated in the experiment."

101 expressed agreement with the statement: "I would like to be part of an experiment again."

102 expressed agreement with the statements: "I have times when I feel angry with other people." "I have times when I feel angry with myself."

93 expressed agreement with the statement: "A Christian person should be able to control his or her anger."

79 expressed agreement with the statement: "A real Christian does not have feelings of anger."

We fully expected the experiment to result in a lively discussion about power and authority roles. We did not expect to raise so many concerns about the problem of anger. Seventy-nine of those participating felt that "a real Christian does not have feelings of anger," but all of them recognized times when they did feel angry.

The experiment had little in common with the work of Zimbardo and Milgram. Careful controls were in place, and most people enjoyed the simulation games. We were careful not to let the simulation become too serious. A simulation game should never be threatening to participants. Nevertheless, the results were significant. Since that time, we have done similar simulations with other church groups, and the results have consistently shown that:

- Even the most committed Christian persons experience feelings of anger toward others *and* toward themselves.

- Many Christians feel guilt over that anger, and many believe that they would not experience anger if they were "fully Christian."

- Many Christians do not know how to deal with their anger in constructive ways.

- Most Christians find a healthy release in being permitted to "act out" their anger under controlled conditions.

Generalizing from specific experiments to society as a whole or even to a particular category of persons carries the risk of error. Experiments can obviously be constructed in such a way as to produce a particular result. Age, sex, race, and other characteristics may cause differences. We have not used the same questionnaire with each group, and the questionnaires have been continuously modified to stimulate discussion by participants rather than to produce data. But some items have been standard on the questionnaires, and the data overall has shown surprising consistency. The groups with which we have worked have been primarily teenage and young adult, white Protestants and Roman Catholics. We have only limited experience with other ethnic groups or with older adults.

THE NATURE OF POWER

Power experiments are like other simulation games. Most people enjoy such experiences. Many people who participate in power experiments are surprised to learn that they can enjoy having power and authority over another person. Many of us do not like to think of ourselves as people who can ENJOY having power.

But we do have power. We have power over our parents. We have power over other members of our families. We have power over the people with whom we work. We have power over people we do not even know. And others have power over us.

It is impossible to simply say that power is GOOD or BAD. Power is the ability to cause change in the world, in other people, in physical objects, or in yourself. Think about the kinds of power that are part of our daily lives.

Ted and Doris argue with each other a lot. Ted feels that Doris is too hard on their son. When she yells at their son or hits him, Ted generally responds by being angry at her. Their son is often confused and has learned that it is safer to ask for things around his father than around his mother. He has also learned that misbehaving when both his parents are present can result in their having a serious disagreement with each other.

Note the amount of power involved in that family situation! Ted and Doris both have power over their son. They can reward him or punish him; praise him or blame him. Doris also has power over Ted and very clearly has the ability to anger him by the manner in which she treats her son. Ted has power over Doris and can ventilate a lot of hostility on her. Their son, while a victim of power in some ways, also possesses power of his own. He can manipulate his parents in many ways. He can talk to his father privately if he wants something that he thinks his mother will not permit. He can misbehave in front of them and thereby cause them to fight. He clearly knows how to upset his mother any time that he wishes to do so.

62

Teresa and Howard have been married for fifteen years. In that period of time, they have developed some predictable routines. Howard works over sixty hours a week, and he feels that his wife should take care of the chores and responsibilities at home. After all, she only works ten hours a week and then does some volunteer work in a hospital and for the school system.

Teresa feels differently. She thinks that her husband does not appreciate how much work it takes to do a good job taking care of the home. She also resents the fact that Howard does not feel her volunteer work is important. She feels that her volunteer work is just as important as his job. She's tired at the end of the day too, and she expects more help around the house.

The sequence of events is always the same: Teresa starts the evening by telling Howard about several things she "hates to nag about but these really need to be done." Howard will act like he is ignoring her for the first part of the evening. Then, as she becomes increasingly insistent, *he will begin to work on the projects. But Teresa is too angry to simply thank him for what he does. She often follows him around the house, yelling at him for not doing a better job and showing him more work that needs to be done.*

Teresa and Howard obviously have a lot of power over each other, and they have learned how to use it for the maximal annoyance to each other. Howard knows that he will do the chores for Teresa, but he delays doing so until she is very angry. Teresa knows that he will eventually do the chores; but his procrastination (delay) angers her, so she keeps yelling at him.

Kate is sixteen and very much resents the power which her parents have over her. She does not want to be told when to come home or where she can go or what she can do. She especially resents the insistence of her parents that they meet all her friends and know something about them.

Her father is currently separated from her mother. Kate feels like their disagreements over how to handle her are part of the problem. Her father was more demanding than her mother. Kate feels her mother is a weak person, and Kate has very little respect for her.

Over the years, Kate has learned that she can turn her back on her mother and block out her mother's attempts at conversation and explanation. Now that her father no longer lives in the same household, Kate frequently copes with her mother's outbursts in this way. Her mother is very frustrated and sometimes gives up.

We don't know that Kate "caused" the separation of her parents. It is doubtful that Kate's behavior was the cause of the separation. If their relationship had been strong, then they would have been able to deal more effectively with Kate. At the same time, Kate may well have helped start some of their disagreements and may have to accept some responsibility for her power over them. They clearly have considerable power over her. Though she can turn her back and ignore them, they still have control over her until she is of legal age to live on her own. Kate has learned that ignoring the conversations of her mother can be an excellent way to get back at her. Her mother does not know how to deal with silence. Since being deserted by her husband, Kate's mother is very sensitive and very much needs the approval of others. She wants more openness from Kate than Kate is willing to give.

Ben has been handicapped all his life. One leg is shorter than the other, and he has never done well in sports.

He had major surgery in an effort to help his situation; but the surgery was very painful and has left him on crutches for several weeks.

Although he has never done well in athletic events, he has always enjoyed participation. His friends have continued to play, leaving him on the sidelines. Ben understands, but part of him wishes they would change routine so that he could participate. He'd enjoy some video games or some other activity that didn't require physical mobility.

People with physical limitations are all about us. Some people have missing limbs. Some are in wheelchairs. Others have diabetes. Some have problems with vision or hearing. Those who are not handicapped have considerable power over those who are. Ben apparently has coped with his handicap fairly well, but his needs are different during his recovery from surgery. While it would not be fair for Ben to expect every activity to be tailored to meet his needs, it is not fair of others to ignore Ben's need for involvement with them. We often exclude those who are handicapped or members of another race or members of another economic class or members of another religion OR . . . .

RATING YOUR OWN POWER

The following list does not cover every possible kind of power, but it does include some of the most common forms. Evaluate your own power by going through the list and placing an **X** on each line to indicate the power which you have in that area. For example, the first item concerns physical strength. If you have better than average physical strength for your age and sex but not as much strength as some people you know, then you might mark your line like this:

Very Little Strength   A Lot of Strength

A person who feels average would place the **X** in the middle of the line. A person who feels considerably below average would place his or her **X** near the left end of the line. Note in each instance that you are asked to indicate how much power you have—not how often you use that power. You may be quite strong physically but do relatively little with that strength.

1. **PHYSICAL STRENGTH** provides the power to move objects; to achieve athletically; and sometimes to force others to do as one wishes.

Very Little Strength   A Lot of Strength

2. **INTELLIGENCE** is a form of power, since it lets us solve problems; better understand the world in which we live; organize our lives; and cope with life.

Low Intelligence   High Intelligence

3. **THE POSSESSION OF MONEY** provides a great deal of power in our society, and many conflicts in our society are the result of some persons having a great deal more money than others. In determining how much money power you have, think about the average amount of spending money that most people your age have. Whether that money comes from an allowance or from a job is not important here.

Less $$$ than Average   More $$$ than Average

4. **THE OPPORTUNITY** to help or hurt, to frustrate or assist other persons is also a form of power. Each day brings us opportunities to be of help to others. Think about the lonely people; the handicapped people; the poor people; the troubled people; and the other people with whom you have contact each day. In a typical week, most people will have contact with at least five or six people to whom they could give significant help. Do you have many opportunities to help or to hurt others?

Very Few Opportunities   Many Opportunities

5. **HAVING FRIENDS AND LOVED ONES** is also a form of power. When our opinions and affection are important to another person, we gain a certain measure of power (or ability to influence or control).

Few Friends & Loved Ones   Many Friends & Loved Ones

6. **KNOWLEDGE** can be a strong form of power. Knowing how to repair a car when others do not is a form of power; knowing how to sew or cook can be a form of power; knowing the secrets of another person can be a form of power. Note that knowledge is not the same as intelligence. Intelligence is the ability to solve problems and to understand things. Knowledge is information which you possess or can easily obtain.

Very Little Knowledge   A Lot of Knowledge

7. **THE ABILITY TO COMMUNICATE** can be an important form of power. Your ability to explain things to other people and to gain the cooperation of other people may make it possible to change or accomplish many things.

Poor Communication Ability   Excellent Communication Ability

POWER COMES FROM GOD

The Scriptures have some strong things to say about power, and some of the Biblical messages clash with our own values. Read through the following statements about power and the related Biblical passages.

1. **All power comes from God.** Real **JOHN 19:1-11.** When Jesus was brought before Pilate, Pilate went to great lengths to make it clear that Christ was in a bad position. "Do you not know that I have power to release you, and power to crucify you?" But Christ denies that claim: "You would have no power over me unless it had been given you from above."

When Job protested the afflictions which he suffered during his time of trial, God reminded him that Job's wisdom and power were as nothing in comparison to God's: "Where were you when I laid the fondation of the earth, [Job]?" You may wish to read **JOB 38:1-18**, in which God reminds Job where the entire created world has come from.

2. **God gives us the power and ability which we need to do what God wills us to do.** Make no mistake about it. God may ask for our best effort—for the gift of 100% of our energy; but God does not ask for the impossible.

Read about the calls of Moses, Jeremiah, and Isaiah. All three felt they were unable to do God's will, but God saw to it that they had the strength or ability which they needed.

- **EXODUS 3-4.** Moses had trouble with his speech and was sure that he would not be taken seriously.

- **JEREMIAH 1:1-7.** Jeremiah felt that he was too young and would not be taken seriously.

- **ISAIAH 6:1-7.** Isaiah felt that he had unclean lips and was not worthy to carry God's word.

3. **Those who would be greatest in the eyes of God are those who are willing to be servants.** Read **MATTHEW 20:20-28** in which Jesus says that those who would be first must be willing to be servants. Also look at the account of the Last Supper in **JOHN 13:1-20**, in which Jesus washes the feet of the disciples.

4. **Physical force is not the way for Christians to resolve most problems.** While Christ did drive the money changers from the temple, He clearly deplored the use of violence under most circumstances. He would not permit violence to be used to save himself when arrested in **MATTHEW 26:47-56**.

5. **Our power and resources should be used to help those in need.** This message is driven home repeatedly in Scripture. And anyone in need becomes our neighbor if we truly believe in Christ.

Read **LUKE 10:25-37.** The story of the Good Samaritan is a classic which most us have heard many times. But the message is still strong: those in need are our neighbors. The people who first heard this parable from our Lord disliked the Samaritan people. Yet Christ makes a Samaritan the hero of the account. Race, religion, nationality, age, sex, have nothing to do with the love which we should show to others.

6. **Forgiveness can be a major form of power in our lives and in the lives of others.** In fact, it is impossible to live happily in this world unless we have the ability to forgive and to accept forgiveness.

Read **LUKE 15:11-32.** The story Prodigal Son is also a familiar one. The youngest son was WRONG. He clearly wasted his inheritance and accepted a lifestyle which was contrary to what he had been taught. But he is accepted and forgiven. God challenges us to do the same in our relationships with others.

7. **We are reminded that, ultimately, judgment belongs not to us but to God.** Read **LUKE 12:4-7** and **MATTHEW 25:31-46.** God's standards are the ones for which we are finally responsible; and if we have been unfaithful to God, the approval of other people is of no worth. Our use of power should always reflect God's will, as best we are able to understand that will.

FOR YOU TO DO

ACTIVITY #1: If you are sharing in this study with a class or group, take time to role play and discuss the situations in THE NATURE OF POWER.

ACTIVITY #2: Complete the RATING YOUR OWN POWER exercise. Share your responses with someone else. Then make resolutions for change in your own use of power.

ACTIVITY #3: Read the Biblical passages given in POWER COMES FROM GOD. Share your feelings about those passages with others. Why is the issue of power so complex? Why is it impossible to separate the issue of anger from the issue of power? Was Christ concerned with power for the sake of power or with power for the sake of good? Why?

ACTIVITY #4: You may enjoy participating in a Power Experiment or a similar simulation game. If you are not interested at all, just skip over this section. We have attempted to provide instructions for simulation games of various intensity and in various settings.

FOR A CLASSROOM: This is for a relatively short power simulation. It can be done in most classroom settings and can be done in as little as thirty minutes. Divide into two groups. Count off by twos. The ones have power, and the twos do not. Division can also be accomplished on the basis of time of arrival, hair color, year in school, and so forth. Use any means you wish, but be careful not to lose too much time in the process of division.

Instructions for Those in Power: You are to consider the other group your prisoners. You are the Interrogation Unit of the Police Department in a small European country. The others are members of an allegedly inferior race who have been arrested for questioning with regard to plots against the government. Before questioning them, you have decided to take ten minutes to display your power over them and to make it clear that they are your prisoners. You do not wish to damage them physically because that could be bad for public relations. You may wish to do things such as: (1) denying them the right to speak; (2) making them stand, sit, or kneel "at attention"; (3) making each person push a penny across the floor with his or her nose (this is **hard** and should not be required of girls wearing dresses); (4) throwing a large number of pencils or crayons on the floor and making your prisoners pick them up with their toes; (5) making your prisoners repeatedly rearrange the furniture in the room; (6) tying the hands of your prisoners.

For those without power: You are living in a small European country in which you are considered members of an inferior race. You have been arrested for questioning by the Interrogation Unit. Although you feel angry at having been arrested, you also know that you must do as ordered, since disobedience may have severe consequences.

70

After the experiment, respond to the items in the appropriate list. Then share your responses in pairs—a person who was in power sharing with a person who was not in power.

SA = Strongly Agree   D = Disagree
A = Agree   SD = Strongly Disagree

Answer if you were in power:

1. _____ I enjoyed being in power.
2. _____ We were too easy on the other team.
3. _____ I was uncomfortable being "mean" to the others.
4. _____ People can easily enjoy having power over others.
5. _____ Under some circumstances, I could enjoy causing pain for another person.
6. _____ Under some circumstances, I could enjoy embarrassing another person.
7. _____ I can remember times I have embarrassed someone else.
8. _____ I can remember times I have caused another person physical or emotional pain.
9. _____ I am frightened by the idea of having power over others.
10. _____ God doesn't give us enough wisdom to handle power properly.
11. _____ The experience would have been fairer if the others had had a turn in power.

Answer if you were not in power:

1. _____ I think the others enjoyed having power over me.
2. _____ The others could have made it a lot tougher.
3. _____ At least part of the experience made me feel embarrassed or angry.
4. _____ People can easily enjoy having power over others.
5. _____ Under some circumstances, I could easily enjoy causing pain for another person.
6. _____ Under some circumstances, I could enjoy embarrassing another person.
7. _____ I can remember times I have caused another person physical or emotional pain.
8. _____ I can remember times I have embarrassed someone else.
9. _____ I am frigtened by the idea of having power over others.
10. _____ God doesn't give us enough wisdom to handle power properly.
11. _____ The experience would have been fairer if we had had a turn in power.

If more time is available, you may wish to reverse the roles.

FOR A RETREAT OR CAMP SETTING: If a longer amount of time is available, all participants should have an opportunity to experience both the "master" and "servant" roles. Depending on the size of your group, divide into an even number of teams. Then the teams will be paired up for the experiment. A team may consist of as few as two people and should not consist of more than five people.

Give some background information to the whole group before beginning the specific planning of the experiment. You may wish to say something like this: "We're going to be doing a simulation game called a Power Experiment. During the course of that game, we'll each experience being in power over others; and we'll also experience being under the power of others. The restrictions will be carefully stated, and we do not intend for anyone to be hurt during the experience. When you are in power, you are responsible for the physical and emotional welfare of those who are your prisoners. In order for the experience to be effective, however, you should not be afraid to use your power. Those who are without power should feel helpless and unfairly treated. You can make your servants do purposeful work for you like cleaning the floor or washing a car or pulling weeds. You can make them do meaningless work like moving piles of rock with their toes; repeatedly rearranging furniture; or picking up cards that you throw on the floor. You can take away their right to speak. You can blindfold them and tie them up. You can make them sing songs to you or do exercises for you or do stupid stunts. You can make them propose love to a water fountain or apologize to a tree. Use your creativity, and remember that the simulation will be most significant if you ENJOY being in power but do NOT enjoy being out of power.

"At the same time, remember that you are responsible for the welfare of those under your power. A counselor/teacher/advisor must approve your plans for the simulation game and also any changes in those plans. These restrictions apply to everyone:

1. You cannot make your servants do anything which poses physical or psychological risk. If in doubt, don't do it.

2. You cannot make your servants remove any clothing except their shoes and socks.

3. If old clothes are available, you can ask your servants to dress foolishly or to wear clothes that they can get dirty. You should not ruin anyone's clothing.

4. You can tie up your prisoners, but be careful not to damage circulation and do not put ropes around anyone's neck!

5. All plans must be written out and approved by a counselor/teacher/advisor. You must also gain approval for any change in plans."

No one should be forced to participate in the simulation.

Then use a time schedule something like this:

- Time for groups to make their plans for their time in power: 30 minutes
- Time for counselors/teachers/advisors to approve plans and take care of questions: 10 minutes
- Time for the first group to be in power: 60-180 minutes
- Time for the second group to be in power: 60-180 minutes
- Time to discuss the experience: 60-90 minutes

The amount of time you should let the groups be in power depends on your setting, the total time available, and the age of the participants. For junior high young people, sixty minutes in power and sixty minutes out of power is long enough. Senior high and young adult groups generally benefit from a longer experience. If you use longer blocks of time, that generally means that one or both groups will be in power during a meal or snack time. If that is the case and your setting permits, you may wish to arrange variation in food between those who are in power and those who are not in power. If an outdoor setting is available, the experiment is generally more enjoyable and can be of longer duration.

You can use many approaches to stimulating discussion. One of the most satisfactory that we have found involves having participants work individually to complete the sentences which follow and then share their responses in small groups—that are not the same as the team in which they did the simulation itself.

1. The worst thing that I had to do when I was out of power was

2. The worst thing that my group or I made our servants do was

3. I enjoyed being in power because

4. I was uncomfortable being in power because

5. If I were to be in power again, I think I could make the experience more effective by

6. Being a prisoner of war or a prisoner in a jail in real life would be different from this experience because

7. People who have no jobs and who have trouble getting food and medical care must feel

8. I can see that it would be easy to abuse having power over other people because

9. I think ventilating your hostility or tension in a simulation like this is a lot better than

10. I would enjoy doing a "real life" power experiment if I could have under my power people like

11. I would not like to be under the power of a person who

12. Power simply means the ability to control or change the behavior or feelings of another person. Physical strength, money, intelligence, knowledge, and affection can all be sources of power. What kinds of real life POWER do these people have over you:

   Parents —

   Teachers —

   Police Officers —

Your best friend(s) —

People you would LIKE to have as close friends —

A member of the opposite sex whom you go out with —

A member of the opposite sex with whom you would LIKE to go out —

Brothers or sisters (if you have any) —

Your employer (if you have one) —

13. What kinds of real life POWER do *you* have over these people:

Parents —

Teachers —

A member of the opposite sex whom you go out with —

Persons who would LIKE to be liked by you —

Your employer (if you have one) —

Brothers or sisters (if you have any) —

14. A Christian should never use his or her power to

15. A Christian should always be willing to use his or her power to

16. A Christian will never use a form of power which

17. A Christian who recognizes money as a form of power will

18. Christ used power to

19. Christ was not willing to use his power to

20. I should change my own use of power by

REWOP: REWOP is "power" spelled backwards, and this game is a kind of backwards approach to looking at power issues! To play the game, you will need to cut out the cards which are printed in the book. The game works best if done in groups of three or four people. It can be done by two people, but it is best not to try the game in groups of more than four. Simply break into small groups if the class or group you are with is a large one. Here are the rules:

1. Arrange the cards into two piles, with **QUESTION** cards in one pile and **PENALTY** cards in the other pile. Shuffle the cards in each pile.

2. Make a decision on the length of time for which you want to play the game. You should play for at least twenty minutes and may enjoy the game for as long as an hour.

3. The person to the right of the individual who shuffled the cards should begin the game by drawing a QUESTION card. That person should read the question aloud to the group, and then decide how he or she will respond to the question. If the person has drawn an EX-PERIENCE QUESTION, then he or she must honestly answer that question for the group. This may involve sharing an experience or a personal opinion. If there are reasons for which the person does not want to answer the question, then he or she must draw a PENALTY card and do whatever the card says. If the person has drawn a FAC-TUAL QUESTION, then he or she will almost certainly want to attempt a response. Another member of the group can look up the correct answer in the REWOP ANSWERS section of this book. If the answer is correct, then the turn passes. If it is incorrect, then the person giving the incorrect answer must draw a PENALTY card and do whatever the card says.

4. Then the game continues, moving to the next person on the right.

5. If you run out of cards before running out of time, simply reshuffle the cards which you have.

6. If there are reasons for which a person is absolutely unwilling to do what is requested on a PENALTY card, then that person may discard that penalty—but must then draw TWO PENALTY cards and do what they say.

7. If a person who has looked up a REWOP ANSWER draws a QUES-TION card and remembers having seen the correct answer to that one, then he or she should draw a new QUESTION card. You can avoid this problem by having one member of the group not participate in the game but function as a moderator and look up the answers for everyone.

8. If you like, you can substitute other QUESTION cards and PENAL-TY cards for the ones provided here. Some groups may want easier questions and penalties; some may want harder questions and penalties.

9. Penalties should normally be performed as soon as the card has been drawn. Note, however, that some penalties continue through the game or for a long enough period of time that the game should continue.

10. You need clothesline or cloth to tie hands and feet for a few of the penalties. If satisfactory material is not available, then those doing penalties requiring them to be tied should hold their hands or feet rigidly in place.

11. Be sure to take time to discuss the experience when you have finished. The questions provided with the previous simulations can easily be used to begin discussion about the REWOP game.

12. CHANGE THE GAME so that it will work well for you! You may like it just as it is, but make changes where they will be helpful.

In 1978, at least ____ million people died as a direct result of too little food.

(a) 5   (b) 10   (c) 15

FACTUAL QUESTION #1

In most developing countries, wealth and power are concentrated in the hands of a few people. In many developing countries 60% of the crop land will be owned by ____% of the landowners.

(a) 2   (b) 20   (c) 33

FACTUAL QUESTION #2

____ of the world's population live in countries with major poverty problems.

(a) 1/4   (b) 1/3   (c) 2/3

FACTUAL QUESTION #3

In the world today, ____ million people suffer from serious malnutrition.

(a) 10   (b) 100   (c) 500

FACTUAL QUESTION #4

The main reason that world population is increasing is _____ .
  (a) birth rates are higher
  (b) average life expectancy is longer
  (c) religions encourage large families

FACTUAL QUESTION #5

Poor people in developing countries tend to have large families because _____ .
  (a) they don't realize how many children suffer from hunger
  (b) they want to continue their family name
  (c) they know that children can help do work and provide security in old age

FACTUAL QUESTION #6

QUESTION CARD

QUESTION CARD

QUESTION CARD

QUESTION CARD

QUESTION CARD

QUESTION CARD

Countries with good educational systems like the United States do not use as much food per person as developing countries.

(a) True   (b) False

FACTUAL QUESTION #7

Natural resources are an important form of power. If the whole world consumed natural gas at the same rate as the United State, natural gas would be gone in ____ years.

(a) 4   (b) 8   (c) 18

FACTUAL QUESTION #8

If your skin is black in color, your chances of being poor if you live in the United States are ____ times as great as if your skin were white.

(a) two   (b) four   (c) six

FACTUAL QUESTION #9

If you are a Native American (American Indian), your chances of being poor if you live in the United States are ____ times as great as if your skin were white.

(a) two   (b) four   (c) six

FACTUAL QUESTION #10

In the United States, one person commits suicide every ____ minutes.

(a) 20   (b) 60   (c) 120

FACTUAL QUESTION #11

Motor vehicles are a significant form of power. Motor vehicle accidents account for ____% of United States accident deaths.

(a) 25   (b) 50   (c) 75

FACTUAL QUESTION #12

QUESTION CARD

QUESTION CARD

QUESTION CARD

QUESTION CARD

QUESTION CARD

QUESTION CARD

Military power is expensive. The annual cost of the United States military budget in terms of taxes to the average family of four is about _____ .

(a) $500   (b) $1000   (c) $2000

FACTUAL QUESTION #13

In a study of nutrition of 619 children from a ghetto area of a major American city, ____% of the children had seriously inadequate diets.

(a) 25   (b) 50   (c) 75

FACTUAL QUESTION #16

Food power may be even more significant than military power in terms of world affairs. Currently, the wealthiest 30% of the world produces ____% of the food and consumes ____% of it.
  (a) 75 50
  (b) 50 30
  (c) 60 . . . 50

FACTUAL QUESTION #14

Some people use their power to kill others. The homicide death rate in the United States is _____ deaths each year per 100,000 of the population.

(a) 1.2   (b) 7.3   (c) 13.4

FACTUAL QUESTION #17

We all have power over our own health. But we may not use that power wisely. ____% of lung cancer patients are cigarette smokers.

(a) 50   (b) 75   (c) 95

FACTUAL QUESTION #15

Money can be a major source of power. Many companies spend a lot of money in advertising to make us buy their products. Each year the toy industry in the United States and Canada will spend over ____ million in television advertising during the Christmas season.

(a) 50   (b) 100   (c) 300

FACTUAL QUESTION #18

QUESTION CARD

QUESTION CARD

QUESTION CARD

QUESTION CARD

QUESTION CARD

QUESTION CARD

More than _____ of American children live below the poverty level.
  (a) 1/10   (b) 1/4   (c) 1/3

FACTUAL QUESTION #19

Faithfulness and loyalty to Christ and others is another form of power. Who denied Christ three times?

FACTUAL QUESTION #22

Which of these racial groups now enjoys the fastest rate of upward mobility in jobs in the United States or Canada?
  (a) whites
  (b) blacks
  (c) Hispanics

FACTUAL QUESTION #20

The love of money can separate us from God. Jesus said that it is as easy for _____ as for a rich man to enter the kingdom of God.

FACTUAL QUESTION #23

If we take the teachings of Christ seriously, then we realize that when we see a person who is hungry or naked or troubled, we are in fact seeing _____ .

FACTUAL QUESTION #21

When Jesus was asked if it was necessary to forgive a person seven times, Jesus replied that it was necessary to forgive _____ .

FACTUAL QUESTION #24

QUESTION CARD

QUESTION CARD

QUESTION CARD

QUESTION CARD

QUESTION CARD

QUESTION CARD

Jesus told the story of a man who was giving a great banquet and who was disappointed when so many people began to send excuses and say they could not come. So the man began to invite those who _____ .

FACTUAL QUESTION #25

According to the New Testament Book of James, what part of the body is a little member that boast of great things (and can cause great harm)?

FACTUAL QUESTION #28

Greater love has no man than this, that a man _____ .

FACTUAL QUESTION #26

Who did Jesus tell that his kingship was not of this world?

FACTUAL QUESTION #29

When Peter saw a man who had been lame since birth and who was begging for money, Peter had no money so he _____ .

FACTUAL QUESTION #27

The power of God was made known in the resurrection. According to the Gospel of John, who was the first person to see Jesus after he was raised from death?

FACTUAL QUESTION #30

QUESTION CARD

QUESTION CARD

QUESTION CARD

QUESTION CARD

QUESTION CARD

QUESTION CARD

Can you remember a time that you said something about another person which wasn't true? Why did you say it? How do you feel about that now?

EXPERIENCE QUESTION

Share a time when you have been extremely angry with your parents. Describe what happened and why you felt as you did.

EXPERIENCE QUESTION

Name a person to whom you should write a letter. Why haven't you done so?

EXPERIENCE QUESTION

Share a time when you have been extremely angry with a close friend. Describe what happened and why you felt as you did.

EXPERIENCE QUESTION

Think of a person about whom you are so angry that you would like REVENGE!! Why are you so angry? What kind of revenge would you like? In what ways would that revenge be helpful or not helpful to you?

EXPERIENCE QUESTION

Can you remember a time that someone else broke your confidence and told something that you wanted kept a secret? How did you feel about what happened? Why do you think the other person did that?

EXPERIENCE QUESTION

QUESTION CARD

QUESTION CARD

QUESTION CARD

QUESTION CARD

QUESTION CARD

QUESTION CARD

Can you remember a time when you broke the confidence of another person and told something that he or she wanted kept a secret? How do you feel about what you did? Why do you think you did it?

EXPERIENCE QUESTION

What do you think is the WORST thing that you have done? Describe that experience. How do you feel about it now?

EXPERIENCE QUESTION

Think of a time when you have hurt an animal or have seen someone else hurt an animal. Was it intentional or unintentional? What responsibilities go with the power that we have over animals?

EXPERIENCE QUESTION

What is the biggest waste of money of which you have been guilty? Why did you waste your money in that way?

EXPERIENCE CARD

Share a time when your parent (or parents) was (were) extremely angry at you. Describe what happened and why they felt as they did.

EXPERIENCE QUESTION

Have you ever had a time that a clerk in a store gave you TOO MUCH change? If so, what did you do about it? If not, what do you think you would do about it?

EXPERIENCE CARD

QUESTION CARD

QUESTION CARD

QUESTION CARD

QUESTION CARD

QUESTION CARD

QUESTION CARD

Drunk drivers are responsible for a very high percentage of the automobile accidents in the United States and Canada. What do you think should be the punishment for driving while intoxicated? for having an accident that kills someone while the person responsible is intoxicated?

EXPERIENCE CARD

Think of a time when you have deliberately avoided contact with a handicapped or deformed person. Why did you do so? How must such experiences affect those who are handicapped or deformed?

EXPERIENCE CARD

How do you feel about the issue of abortion? Under what circumstances, if any, should abortion be permitted?

EXPERIENCE CARD

Tell how you feel about cigarette and cigar smokers being permitted to smoke in public places like restaurants and lobbies. Should that be permitted? Why, or why not?

EXPERIENCE CARD

Think of a time when you have genuinely forgiven someone who wronged you. Describe what happened. How did your forgiveness affect your relationship with that person?

EXPERIENCE CARD

Under what circumstances, if any, would you be willing to take the life of another person?

EXPERIENCE CARD

QUESTION CARD

QUESTION CARD

QUESTION CARD

QUESTION CARD

QUESTION CARD

QUESTION CARD

Think of a time when you have done something dishonest (like shoplifting or cheating on a test or . . .). Why did you do what you did?

EXPERIENCE CARD

Have your hands tied behind your back for the rest of the game. If nothing is available with which to tie them, keep them crossed behind your back.

PENALTY CARD

Think of a time when someone else has forgiven you for something you did which was wrong. Describe what happened. How did that forgiveness affect your relationship with that person?

EXPERIENCE CARD

Stand at attention while you count backwards from 500. If you leave out any numbers, you must start over.

PENALTY CARD

Have your feet tied together for the rest of the game. If nothing is available with which to tie them, cross your ankles and keep them crossed for the remainder of the game.

If you have to do another penalty which requires movement, then your feet may be untied long enough to do that penalty.

PENALTY CARD

Hold your left arm in the air until it is your turn again.

PENALTY CARD

PENALTY CARD	QUESTION CARD
PENALTY CARD	QUESTION CARD
PENALTY CARD	PENALTY CARD

BAD NEWS CARD. Draw two more penalty cards and do whatever they require.

PENALTY CARD

Pretend that the person on your left is a "Moonie" (member of the Unification Church). Spend the next three minutes explaining why that person should leave the Unification Church.

PENALTY CARD

You cannot talk for the rest of the game except for the purpose of answering the questions which you draw or doing the penalties you draw.

PENALTY CARD

Give a back rub for three minutes to the person on your right. If that person does not feel it was a good back rub, then he or she can tickle you for one minute.

PENALTY CARD

For three minutes, do whatever exercises the person on your right orders.

PENALTY CARD

GOOD NEWS CARD. You do not have to do a penalty.

PENALTY CARD

PENALTY CARD

PENALTY CARD

PENALTY CARD

PENALTY CARD

PENALTY CARD

PENALTY CARD

Push a penny twenty feet across the floor using your nose.

If you are a girl and wearing a dress, you do NOT do this penalty. Instead, draw and do another penalty.

PENALTY CARD

Confess to a chair your great love and affection for it. Your confession of love must last for at least three minutes.

PENALTY CARD

Go change in privacy. You must put your clothes on backwards for the rest of the game. (Shirt buttoned up the back instead of the front; pants on backwards; socks turned inside out, right shoe on the left foot and left shoe on the right foot).

If you cannot do this, draw and do TWO other penalties.

PENALTY CARD

Dance for three minutes without music or a partner.

PENALTY CARD

Stick your tongue out for the next three minutes.

PENALTY CARD

Hold your left foot in your right hand for the next two turns.

PENALTY CARD

PENALTY CARD

PENALTY CARD

PENALTY CARD

PENALTY CARD

PENALTY CARD

PENALTY CARD

Get tickled for sixty seconds by the player on your left.

PENALTY CARD

Hold your arms straight up in the air for the next three minutes.

PENALTY CARD

Take off your shoes and socks for the rest of the game.

PENALTY CARD

GOOD NEWS CARD. You do not have to do a penalty.

PENALTY CARD

Spend three minutes singing a song of your choice loudly and out of tune.

PENALTY CARD

Pat your head with your right hand for the next two turns.

PENALTY CARD

PENALTY CARD

PENALTY CARD

PENALTY CARD

PENALTY CARD

PENALTY CARD

PENALTY CARD

GOOD NEWS CARD. You do not have to do a penalty.

PENALTY CARD

For the next turn, you must sit holding your right ankle in your left hand and your left ankle in your right hand.

PENALTY CARD

Walk backwards around the room three times.

PENALTY CARD

Spend the next three minutes telling the person on your right what a marvelous, fantastic, great person he or she is. If that person does not agree that you did a good job, draw a new penalty card.

PENALTY CARD

The person on your left has permission to tickle your feet for one minute.

PENALTY CARD

Rub your head with your right hand at the same time you rub your stomach with your left hand. Continue this for two more turns. Someone else can read your next two cards to you. If you have to stop to do another penalty, then start over again after you've done the penalty.

PENALTY CARD

PENALTY CARD

PENALTY CARD

PENALTY CARD

PENALTY CARD

PENALTY CARD

PENALTY CARD

Write the words "I FEEL DUMB"
two times by holding a pencil between your toes. You can only use
your hands to initially place the pencil between your toes and to place a
sheet of paper on the floor.

PENALTY CARD

BAD NEWS CARD FOR THE
PERSON ON YOUR LEFT. That
person must draw a penalty card
and do whatever it says.

PENALTY CARD

PENALTY CARD

PENALTY CARD

REWOP ANSWERS

1. b	4. c	7. b	10. c	13. c
2. b	5. b	8. a	11. a	14. c
3. c	6. c	9. b	12. b	15. c

16. c   19. b

17. b   20. a

18. b

21. Christ

22. Peter

23. a camel to go thru the eye of a needle

24. seventy times seven

25. were poor, blind, and lame

26. lay down his life for his friends

27. healed him in the name of Christ

28. the tongue

29. Pilate

30. Mary

PART II

DO SOMETHING CONSTRUCTIVE

This section of the book challenges you to begin doing something about those feelings of anger. We're providing twenty-eight days worth of regular devotions and exercises designed to help you:

- Better understand your feelings of anger.
- Handle that anger more constructively.
- Learn how to feel better about yourself.
- Learn how to feel better about other people.
- Channel some of your anger and assertiveness into making the world a better place in which to live.
- Help you grow closer to God.

Though it is not absolutely necessary, you will find this experience most helpful if you can visit with a class, a group, or just another person on the first, eighth, fifteenth, and twenty-second days.

You will need to set aside a few minutes at the beginning of each day or at the end of each day to do the devotions, record your reflections in the journal writing space provided, and lift your concerns to God in prayer.

DAY ONE — WEEK ONE

These are activities to do in a group or by yourself. The focus this week will be on better understanding God's love for all people—and for you in particular.

1. Read **MATTHEW 1-2.** If you are doing this study in the spring or summer, you may feel strange reading the Christmas story! But remember how central the Christmas story is to the roots of our faith and to the reality of God's love for us. Write down your responses to these questions. If possible, share those responses with others.

    A. WHY do you think God came to humanity in the person of Jesus? Note that the name *Emmanuel* means "God with us."

    B. Why would the story of Christ's birth have a different meaning if he had been born into a wealthy, prestigious home?

    C. Why does wealth have nothing to do with one's worth in the eyes of God?

2. Identify the things in life for which you are most thankful. That list may include people, things, opportunities, places, skills, animals, historical events, personality traits, and so forth. Make a list here of the ten things for which you are most thankful. Share that list with others.

    1.   6.

    2.   7.

    3.   8.

    4.   9.

    5.   10.

3. Think of the TWO people for whose lives you are most grateful. Write down their names and something about why you are grateful for them. Share your feelings with someone else.

    1.

    2.

4. Think of a person you like, who lives near you, whom you have not visited with for several weeks. Write down the name of that person. RESOLVE that sometime this week you are going to telephone that person or visit that person.

5. NOW write down the FIVE BEST THINGS ABOUT YOURSELF. Share those with someone else, and give God thanks in prayer for the life He has given you.

1.

2.

3.

4.

5.

We know God's love through many experiences—especially through good friends.

DAY TWO

Read **1 JOHN 4:7-12.** Think about the day you have just finished. Think about the people with whom you had contact; the places you went; and the things you did. Record here at least three ways in which you experienced the love of God during the day. Then give God thanks in prayer.

DAY THREE

Read **1 JOHN 4:13-21.** Then think about the last person who made you angry—whether that happened today, yesterday, last week, or last month. No matter how much you dislike that person, think about how you would feel toward that person if you truly saw him or her as a child of God. Record here BOTH the good and the bad feelings which you have toward that person. Then share those with God in prayer.

DAY FOUR

Read **1 JOHN 5:1-5.** Now do an exercise which at first may seem artificial. Close your eyes and repeat to yourself TEN TIMES: "I am a child of God." THEN think of a person you love a great deal; close your eyes; and repeat to yourself TEN TIMES: "_____ is a child of God." THEN think of someone you find it difficult to get along with; close your eyes; and repeat to yourself TEN TIMES: "_____ is a child of God." Record here some of the ways in which it is HARD and some of the ways in which it is EASY to see yourself and others as the children of God. Share those reflections with God in prayer.

We are all children of God, but it is not always easy to love God's children!!

DAY FIVE

Read **ROMANS 8:12-18.** The fact that we are God's children does not mean that life will always be easy. In truth life was not easy for Christ. Christ's earthly existence ended on a cross where he was forsaken by many who had followed him. Record here some of the things that make your life hard at this particular time. Then offer those to God in prayer, seeking his love and strength.

DAY SIX

Read **1 CORINTHIANS 13:1-13.** These words are among the best known in the Bible. Think about why it is more important to be loved and to love others than to have financial success or popularity or great achievements or anything else. Record here some of the ways in which your life would really be improved if you could live fully aware of the importance of love. Share those thoughts with God in prayer.

DAY SEVEN

Read **1 JOHN 2:1-11.** Love has little meaning if it is never translated into action. That is why the Scriptures so repeatedly talk about the importance of obeying God's commandments. To say that one loves God but to lie to others, to steal from others, to manipulate others, or to hurt others does not work. If we love God, we work to do God's will. That does not mean that we achieve perfection, but it does mean that we try to improve our ability at expressing God's love. Rate yourself from *1* (low) to *5* (high) in terms of keeping God's commandments in relationship to other people by:

_____ telling the truth to other people.

_____ helping other people when they are in trouble.

_____ forgiving other people when they wrong you.

_____ seeking the forgiveness of others when you have wronged them.

_____ not taking unfair advantage of someone else.

_____ helping others feel good about themselves.

On DAY ONE, you were asked to identify someone close to you with whom you had not visited in several weeks. Have you visited with that person this week? Why, or why not? Record here some of your thoughts on that visit or on the fact that you failed to make the visit. Why is it difficult to make ourselves do the things which would help us feel better about other people and about our own lives? Share your thoughts with God in prayer.

DAY EIGHT — WEEK TWO

These are activities to do in a group or by yourself. The focus this week will be on doing things which will help you feel better about yourself and about others.

1. Read **LUKE 10:25-37.** These verses contain the story of the GOOD SAMARITAN and also contain the words of the GREAT COMMAND-MENT. Note that the people who first heard this story did not like the Samaritan people. Thus it is of special significance that Jesus made the Samaritan the hero of the story. Record your reflections to these questions, and share them with someone else if possible:

A. If Jesus were to retell the story of the Good Samaritan in our own time, what kind of person might he make the hero or heroine instead of the Samaritan? Why?

B. Why is it so easy to hurry through life and fail to be of help to others?

C. How do you feel about yourself when you actually take the time to help another person?

2. This week you should attempt to do something every day which will help you feel better about yourself and about others. Identify people with whom or for whom you could do each of the following, and write their names in the space provided:

Day Nine: Share a compliment with someone you know and like. Who would be a good person? _____

Day Ten: Share a compliment with someone you do not especially like. Who would be a good person? _____

Day Eleven: Write a letter to someone who would like to hear from you. To whom will you write? _____

Day Twelve: Think of someone who has given you a great deal of help at some time in the last year. Write a letter of thanks to that person. To whom will you write? _____

Day Thirteen: Think of someone in your neighborhood, at a nursing home, or at school who is lonely. Visit that person. If you have trouble thinking of someone, get a name from a minister or someone else who is familiar with your community. Whom will you visit? _____

Day Fourteen: Plan to do something with a person or persons you like. Take a hike, go swimming, have a coke, whatever you want. What will you do?_____

With whom will you do it? _____

3. Identify three situations in which you normally get angry. These may include dealing with particular teachers or an employer; certain predictable events in your family; interaction with clerks in stores; or exchanges with people your own age. Write those situations down:

   1.

   2.

   3.

NOW decide which of those three situations has the best potential for being changed by your being KIND to the person or persons involved. If none of the situations have that potential, face that reality. What might first steps be on changing such a situation?

Be kind to yourself! Do something with people you like.

DAY NINE

Read again **LUKE 10:25-37.** WHY do you think Jesus summarized the law in this way? WHY did He make a Samaritan the hero of the story? Record your reflections here. Also record the kinds of people whom you find it most difficult to see as NEIGHBORS. Then share those thoughts with God in prayer.

REMEMBER that this is a day to share a compliment with someone you know and like. Record what you did (or plan to do) here:

DAY TEN

Read **MATTHEW 5:43-48.** The tax collectors were greatly disliked in the time of Christ. Christ points out that those who are only kind to the people they like are no better than tax collectors or other selfishly motivated people. Think about some of the people you find it difficult to like. Remember that showing Christ's love and concern to someone does not mean approving of what that person does. Christ reached out to tax collectors, but Christ did not approve of the harsh means by which some of them raised money for themselves and the government. Record here some of your reflections on the importance of treating others well. Share your thoughts with God in prayer.

REMEMBER that this is a day to share a compliment with someone you do not especially like. Record what you did (or plan to do) here:

DAY ELEVEN

Read **1 CORINTHIANS 1:1-9.** Letters were an especially important means of communication for the early church. Paul was very much concerned about the people in the church at Corinth, but distances made it impossible to travel as far or as often as Paul would have liked. Thus letters were a means of sharing his concern. Record some of your thoughts on how you feel when you receive mail or phone calls. Give God thanks for the many ways in which we can communicate with others.

REMEMBER that this is a day to write a letter to someone who would like to hear from you. Record what you did (or plan to do) here:

DAY TWELVE

Read **PHILIPPIANS 1:1-11.** Paul obviously expresses special appreciation to the Philippians for their partnership in his work and for their concern for him. All of us are deeply helped by the efforts of others—by our families, teachers, friends, and even by people we encounter but once or twice in our lives. Yet we seldom take time to say THANKS for what others have done for us. Record your reflections on what some others have done for you and on how you feel when someone expresses appreciation to you. Then give God thanks for those people and those experiences.

REMEMBER that this is a day to write a letter to someone who has given you a great deal of help at some time in the last year. Record what you did (or plan to do) here:

DAY THIRTEEN

Read **JAMES 2:14-17.** Many of us do a better job of talking about our faith than of acting on our faith. The world is filled with people in need—some have physical needs for food, clothing, and shelter which go unmet. Others need companionship, concern, and a sense of their own importance as children of God. Record here a few of the things you would do differently in your own life IF you put your faith to work. Then offer those concerns to God in prayer.

REMEMBER that this is a day to visit someone who is lonely. If you cannot get that done today, then be sure to set a time for doing so. Record here what you did (or plan to do):

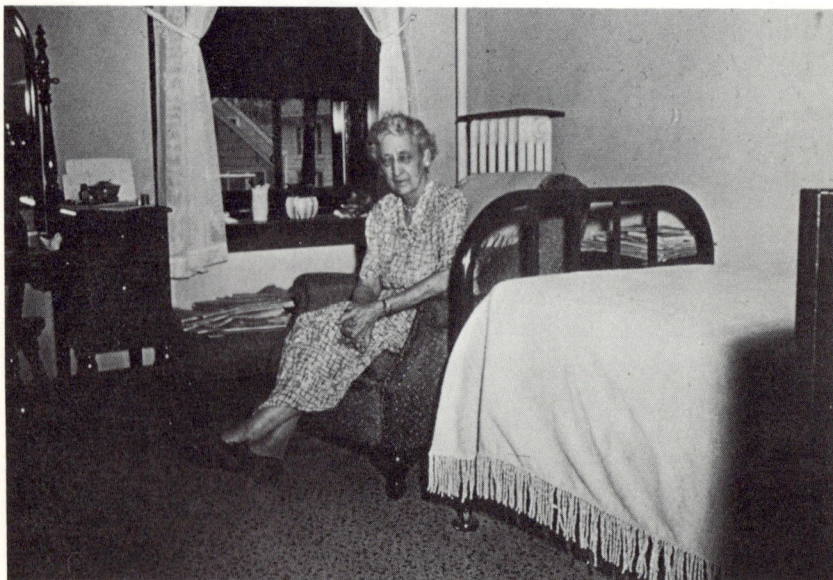

Visit someone who is lonely.

Do something you like with people you like.

DAY FOURTEEN

Read **1 CORINTHIANS 12:12-21.** This famous passage compares the body of Christ, which is the church, to the human body. Each part or member is of importance to the proper functioning of the whole body. What are the particular things which you have to contribute to the body of Christ, which is the church? What things are you unable to do that others can do? Record your reflections here, and then share them with God in prayer.

REMEMBER that this is a day to do something you enjoy with people you like. If you cannot get that done today, then be sure to set a time for doing so. Record here what you did (or plan to do):

DAY FIFTEEN — WEEK THREE

The past two weeks have involved you in activities to help you feel better about yourself, about others, and about God. Working hard on such activities almost inevitably makes it easier to deal with anger and conflict. This week challenges you to improve the way you handle your feelings of anger. After all, those feelings are going to arise no matter how good you feel about yourself and about others! The activities for this day are to be done in a group or by yourself.

1. Read **MATTHEW 5:21-26** and **JOHN 2:13-16.** It's hard to fit those passages together! In one passage, Christ tells us that it is wrong to have negative feelings toward others and to express those feelings. In the other passage, Christ drives the money-changers from the temple. Write down responses to these questions, and then share them with others:

A. Note that in the passage in Matthew, Christ is sharing His teachings with a group assembled to listen to him. In the passage in John, Christ has discovered open disrespect of God's house. Those who sold animals for sacrifice often overcharged people and used a worship setting for their personal profit. In what ways would the difference in situations explain the difference between Christ's words in Matthew and his actions in John?

B. What real life situations seem to you most like those to which Christ made reference in the Matthew passage? Why is it wrong to attack the self worth of others?

C. What real life situations are most like those to which Christ made reference in the John passage? Why is it wrong to keep silent in the face of obvious injustice?

2. Although Christ does not violate the rights of others and will not use violence to save himself when arrested, He has no hesitation in standing up for what is right and in refusing to be manipulated by the Pharisees and by others. His behavior in many ways follows the ASSERTIVE style which was described in the first and second chapters of the book. Identify THREE situations in the past month in which you should have been ASSERTIVE instead of SILENT or in which you should have been ASSERTIVE instead of AGGRESSIVE. Record those situations, and think about how you might have handled them differently.

   1.

   2.

   3.

3. If you are meeting with a class or group, you may find it helpful to act out or role play some of the situations which you have not handled as effectively as you would like.

Another approach to practicing assertiveness, if you have trouble being assertive, would be to do a power experiment or play the REWOP game from the chapter on power.

Remember that the "power" role in a power simulation is most helpful to those who have trouble being assertive enough in real life situations. If your problem is one of being too aggressive, it may be more beneficial for you to be OUT of power than in power during a simulation! Structure the experience in whatever way will be helpful.

4. RESOLVE to work in the week ahead on being **MORE ASSERTIVE** or **LESS AGGRESSIVE**—depending on the change which you most need to make. Record your progress on that goal each day!

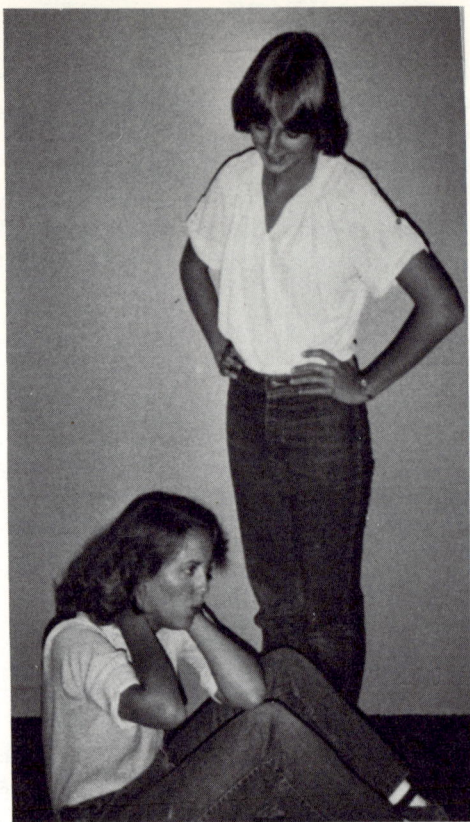

Properly done, a power simluation can be of special help to people who normally have trouble being assertive enough.

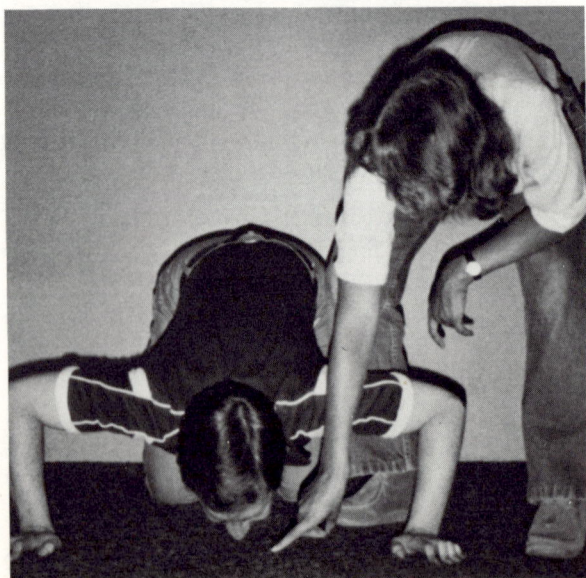

DAY SIXTEEN

Read **MATTHEW 5:1-12.** In these verses, Christ reverses many of our traditional norms and values. The word which is often translated as "blessed" is a Greek word which can also be translated "happy" or "how happy." Record your reflections on the possibility that meekness, mercy, and mourning can result in happiness in God's sight. Offer your thought to God in prayer.

How are you doing on your goal of being **MORE ASSERTIVE** or **LESS AGGRESSIVE** this week? Make notes here:

DAY SEVENTEEN

Read **MATTHEW 5:5** and **EXODUS 2:11-15** and **8:1-7.** Many people feel that the word MEEK means the same thing as WEAK, but that is not true! Moses is described as a meek man, but Moses is in no way a weak man! Moses had the courage and strength to kill an Egyptian who was beating a servant and to face Pharaoh in God's name. Few people in history have been so brave or so assertive! Being meek means having a sense of one's own identity and worth. A person who is genuinely meek has self-confidence and does not have to go through life enforcing his or her will on others. Record some of your reflections on how your life would be different if you had more confidence in yourself. Seek God's help in prayer in having more confidence in yourself AND more confidence in God's ability to strengthen you.

How are you doing on your goal of being **MORE ASSERTIVE** or **LESS AGGRESSIVE** this week? Make notes on your progress (or lack of progress):

DAY EIGHTEEN

Read **MATTHEW 5:13-16.** Others will not know of our faith in Christ unless we show that faith by our words and by our actions. If our words proclaim Christ but our actions are in violation of God's commandments, people will not take our words seriously. Record here some of the things that you should do that your "light" might be more visible to others. Share those thoughts with God in prayer.

How are you doing on your goal of being **MORE ASSERTIVE** or **LESS AGGRESSIVE** this week? Record your progress here:

DAY NINETEEN

Read **MATTHEW 6:16-33.** Many of us are filled with anxiety about money; about how well others like us; about how we look; about how we feel; and so forth!! We waste a great deal of energy with anxiety. Record some of the things about which you are worried or concerned. Then offer those concerns to God in prayer.

Record your progress on your goal of being **MORE ASSERTIVE** or **LESS AGGRESSIVE:**

God does know how to care for us and wills that we care for others.

DAY TWENTY

Read **MATTHEW 7:7-12.** We need have no doubt about it. God does love us and care for us. If we could accept that reality, we would find it far easier to like ourselves and far easier to get along with others. Record some of the changes you would make in your own life if you lived fully conscious of God's love.

Record here your progress in being **MORE ASSERTIVE** or **LESS AGGRESSIVE:**

DAY TWENTY-ONE

Read **MATTHEW 7:24-27.** Jesus spoke these words at the end of the Sermon on the Mount (or at least at the end of the Sermon as we have it recorded; the actual Sermon may have been considerably longer!). What is the real foundation of your life? Your own happiness? Your desire to be accepted by others? Your concern to be professionally successful? Your desire to be loved by your parents? Why are such goals generally inadequate during the storms of life? Record some of your reflections here, and then seek God's help in building a firmer foundation for your life.

Record here how your work this week has gone on the goal of being **MORE ASSERTIVE** or **LESS AGGRESSIVE.**

DAY TWENTY-TWO — WEEK FOUR

This will be your last week of devotional work using **A PRIMER FOR ANGRY CHRISTIANS**, but we hope it will not be your last week working on issues of anger and power. In fact, we hope you may select some projects that will continue for a long time to come!!

The activities for this day are to be done in a group or by yourself.

1. Read **MATTHEW 25:31-46.** These are among the strongest words of our Lord. In this passage, Jesus identifies Himself with the hungry and the oppressed of the world. He also says that the manner in which we have treated those who were less fortunate will be directly related to God's evaluation of our lives. Complete the following statements in your own words. If possible, share your responses with others.

A. I am afraid that I have failed to see Christ in

B. I sometimes find it hard to see Christ in the poor and oppressed because

C. If I really took this passage seriously, I would

2. There are some issues about which one should get upset! Part of the problem with society today is that so many of us waste energy getting upset about the wrong things! There are many issues of vital importance to the future of our world and to the welfare of many people that are literally begging for our involvement.

Let your anger or your sense of outrage become the force which motivates you to do something positive about the pressing concerns of our time. This section provides you with information about several issues with which you may want to get involved because of your commitment to God as revealed in Jesus Christ. At this time, our suggestion is that you personally pick ONE issue with which you would like to be involved. If you are meeting with a class or group, the class or group as a whole may also want to pick an issue for continued involvement.

Try weighting each of these possibilities from *1* (low) to *5* (high) in terms of your interest in the issue. If you are with a group, the scores can be added to see what comes out on top. All the issues are worthwhile; the decision concerns where YOU most want to put YOUR energy as an individual and (perhaps) as a group.

_____ The needs of the physically handicapped. Literally millions of people in our country suffer from permanent physical handicaps. This is an important individual issue because many of those who are handicapped desperately need the friendship and outreach of those who are not. There is a sense in which ALL people are handicapped or disabled in some way, but many of us are extremely uncomfortable around those whose physical handicaps are extremely visible.

This is also an important issue for our churches. Persons with severe handicaps are generally not in church on Sunday morning. Many of our churches are not accessible for wheelchairs or for persons with other mobility problems. Other churches make no provision for signing for those who are deaf. Most churches have not learned how to relate to the physically handicapped in a normal way—recognizing the human being rather than the disability.

The Division of Vocational Rehabilitation in your area may be able to help you identify the number of handicapped persons in your community. A phone survey to see what facilities and services are available through churches could be another helpful starting point.

Harold Wilke's *Creating the Caring Congregation* can be a valuable resource for churches wanting to reach out to the handicapped.

_____ The shortage of food and other physical necessities is a painful reality of the world today. A few countries, including the United States and Canada, control most of the world's food supply. Ways have not yet been found to insure that ALL people have enough to eat. The REWOP game included some depressing statistics on the magnitude of world hunger, and those statistics were conservative.

This picture was taken in Haiti. People do live in housing this poor. They also die in such housing as a direct result of too little food and chronic malnutrition.

You can readily get involved in local hunger needs. Your minister can give you some information on local programs. The county supervisor and the nearest Salvation Army can also provide helpful information. If your community does not already have a canned food pantry for emergency assistance, your church might want to begin one. If such a pantry already exists, then you may wish to help keep it supplied.

Two ecumenical groups dealing with hunger issues can give you good help in influencing legislation that relates to food concerns. Write to **IMPACT**, 110 Maryland Avenue, NE, Washington, D.C. 20002 or to **BREAD FOR THE WORLD**, 207 E. 16th Street, New York, New York 10003.

_____ Child abuse is a significant problem in many communities. Accurate statistics on child abuse are hard to find because so many cases go unreported. It is certain that preventative programs are desperately needed. Contact your local state social services agency.

_____ Human rights are routinely violated in many countries of the world. Political prisoners, especially in African and South American countries, have few legal rights. Accounts of torture, murder, and inhuman experimentation have come from some of these countries. If you would like to help influence change in these areas, get on the mailing list for **AMNESTY INTERNATIONAL**, USA, 2112 Broadway, New York, New York 10023.

_____ The quality of much television programming makes us cringe! TV shows often present values in radical conflict both with the Christian faith and with the welfare of any people watching television. One of the best approaches to dealing with this issue is through Television Awareness Training. Write to **MEDIA ACTION RESEARCH CENTER**, 475 Riverside Drive, New York, New York 10027 for information about programs in your area.

_____ Our own lifestyles waste needed resources for the rest of the world. Those of us in the United States and Canada throw away too many tin cans, eat too much meat, consume too much energy, and destroy too much paper. If you would like to deal more intensely with this issue from a Christian perspective, order the C-4 RESOURCES book **Repairing Christian Lifestyles** from **C-4 RESOURCES**, P.O. Box 27, Sidell, Illinois, 61876.

_____ Race Relations continue to be strained in most parts of the country. While the issues concerning racial identity were once primarily focused on white/black relations, the increasing number of Spanish-speaking persons brings some new issues in terms of tolerance and acceptance of diversity. Start doing what you can in your own school, community, and church to improve racial relations.

_____ Male/female relationships have been going through considerable change in our society. Some of the once popular but never good images of what it means to be a man and what it means to be a woman have disappeared. These changes have not been without impact on family life and on the economy. You may wish to visit with others your age about the direction in which the world seems headed and about ways of insuring fair treatment of both men and women in employment decisions and policies. You may also wish to consider involvement in a RAPE HOTLINE service for your area. Women's liberation has not eliminated the crime of rape, and it remains one of the worst crimes that can be directed against another human being.

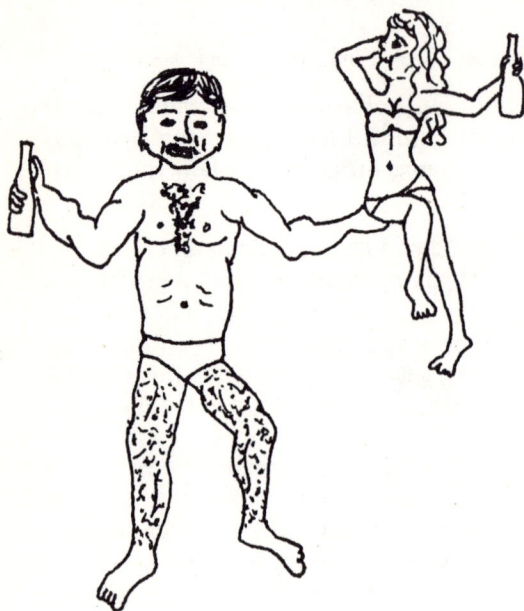

The list could obviously be continued—almost without limit. Pollution, prison reform, endangered wildlife, alternative Christmas celebration, and many other concerns can be legitimate recipients of your time, energy, and material resources. YOU need to decide where YOU want to be involved. BE WARNED! Change in areas such as those discussed in this section comes very slowly. Prepare to be frustrated by your first several efforts to change the way things are done in our society.

3. You CANNOT do everything. If you have not done so yet, MAKE A CHOICE. Decide on ONE issue you will tackle as an individual and (perhaps) on ONE you will tackle as a group. Write them here, and begin to lay concrete plans for beginning. You should make at least some initial steps this week.

DAY TWENTY-THREE

Read **MATTHEW 19:23-30.** Note that Jesus does not say that it is impossible for a rich man to enter the kingdom of heaven. But Jesus makes it clear that it will be very hard and only by the grace of God. No matter how much one accumulates, it simply can't be taken through the Pearly Gates!

Record some of your reflections on the reasons why people want to accumulate wealth so desperately. Then share those concerns with Christ in prayer.

Record your progress (or lack of progress) on the major goal which you set for this week:

DAY TWENTY-FOUR

Read **JAMES 2:14-16.** Martin Luther considered the Book of James an "epistle of straw" because of its discussion about salvation by works. Whether one says that we are saved by faith or by works, a simple truth remains. If our relationships with God are strong, then our works will reflect our faith. Record some of your own thoughts on the importance of translating words into action. Share those concerns with God in prayer.

Record your progress (or lack of progress) on the major goal which you set for this week.

DAY TWENTY-FIVE

Read **JAMES 3:1-12.** This section talks about the evils of the tongue and the troubles into which we travel because we do not control what we say. Record some of the problems you have had in expressing yourself to others and in not alienating others. Then offer these concerns to God in prayer.

Record your progress (or lack of progress) on your major goal for the week:

DAY TWENTY-SIX

Read **ISAIAH 55:1-8** and **58:1-9.** Simply going through the rituals was not satisfactory. The Israelites are condemned in these passages for seeking their own goals and doing religious rituals without thought for their actions. In what ways does the failure of many churches to respond to local and world hunger needs made our worship seem artificial? In what ways is it hopeless to expect that we will ever respond adequately to those needs? Record some of your thoughts, and then seek God's help.

The week is going fast! **Record** your progress on your major goal for the week:

"I have sworn upon the altar of God eternal hostility against every form of tyranny over the mind of man."

—Thomas Jefferson

DAY TWENTY-SEVEN

Read **JOHN 13:1-20.** This account of the Last Supper portrays Jesus washing the feet of the disciples. If we are to be God's leaders in the world, then we must be ready to humble ourselves in service to others. What would it mean to take this passage seriously within your own life? within the life of the church? within the world? Record your thoughts, and seek God's help in prayer.

Record your progress on your goal for the week:

DAY TWENTY-EIGHT

Read **GENESIS 1-2.** God is the power behind all that we know. There is no power greater than God, and there is no power that does not come ultimately from God. There is also no holder of power who is not ultimately accountable before God. The world does not belong to us to do with as we please. Our lives do not belong to us to use selfishly as we wish. Those whose lives touch our own are the children of God and merit respect and love because of that relationship. Anger as we know it may one day pass away. Power as we know it may one day pass away. But the creative, redemptive love of God as revealed in Jesus Christ will hold for all eternity. Record your thoughts on that reality, and then offer God thanks for the gift of life—and for the gifts of anger and power when they are used responsibly.

This is the last day of journal writing in this book, but it is probably not the last day of work on your project. We hope you have found a meaningful project that can be a focus of your energy for years to come. **Record** your progress on your goal here:

If you would like other information about materails from C-4 RESOURCES or if you would like to share comments about this book, you can write to:

C-4 RESOURCES
P.O. Box 27
Sidell, Illinois 61876

C-4 materials are normally available only by direct mail. Only a few selected religious bookstores carry them. C-4 RESOURCES is a private religious research and publishing organization. We publish a free newsletter called **YOUTH MINISTRY UPDATE** and would be glad to put you on our mailing list for that.

A large number of secular publications deal with assertiveness, anger, aggression, and other related topics. If you would like suggestions for further reading, write to us at the above address. The concept of "clear thinking" has been developed by many people. We find the rational-emotive therapy books of Albert Ellis and Paul Hauck especially helpful. Hauck writes from a more Christian perspective than Ellis. Write to us at the above address if you want suggestions for further study in any of these areas.